Mind Mirroring: The Magic of the Empty Chair

Cort Curtis, Ph.D.

Published by Cort Curtis, Ph.D., 2023.

While every precaution has been taken in the preparation of this book, the publisher assumes no responsibility for errors or omissions, or for damages resulting from the use of the information contained herein.

MIND MIRRORING: THE MAGIC OF THE EMPTY CHAIR

First edition. December 14, 2023.

Copyright © 2023 Cort Curtis, Ph.D..

ISBN: 979-8223552536

Written by Cort Curtis, Ph.D..

Table of Contents

Dedicated to the brave voyagers of the inner realm, pursuing self-growth and spiritual enlightenment:

"Mind Mirroring: The Magic of the Empty Chair" is a tribute to you, the seekers and healers, embarking on the profound journey to unlock your ultimate potential.

Within these pages lies a route to healing, self-discovery, and transformation. May you discover immense peace and joy as you align with your innermost truths and embrace the fullness of your being.

Introduction

In the quiet recesses of the mind, a continuous performance unfolds—an intimate conversation that is heard by an audience of one. This ceaseless stream, known as the "inner monologue" or "inner dialogue," is the mind's own theater. On this private stage, thoughts, feelings, debates, and rehearsals for life's myriad scenarios play out. It is a dialogue that often runs like an undercurrent beneath the surface of our social interactions, an inaudible discourse that shapes our perception of reality, governs our responses, and reflects our deepest selves.

For some, this inner monologue is a gentle whisper, a reflective adviser offering wisdom and guidance through life's complexities. For others, it can be a critical voice, challenging every decision, casting doubt, or bolstering confidence. The nature of this internal conversation is as diverse as humanity itself, influenced by individual personalities, past experiences, cultural backgrounds, and the unique wiring of each person's brain.

Our inner monologue is a crucial component of our consciousness. It is where decisions are weighed, risks are assessed, and emotions are processed. This inner voice can be our greatest ally or a formidable adversary, pushing us toward growth or pulling us into rumination. It narrates our personal stories and, in many ways, becomes the author of our life's narrative, shaping our sense of identity and our understanding of who we are.

Understanding this internal dialogue is not just an exercise in introspection; it is a gateway to mastering one's own mind. Through this understanding, we can learn to direct this dialogue, to cultivate a more compassionate and empowering voice within. And perhaps, with this mastery, we can transform the very nature of our internal conversations, turning them into a powerful tool for personal and spiritual growth—a concept that we will explore deeply in the pages of "Mind Mirroring: The Magic of the Empty Chair."

As we embark on this journey, we'll explore the psychological and spiritual foundations of the inner monologue, its impact on our lives, and the ways we can harness it through the modified gestalt two-chair technique. We will not merely be observers of this internal performance but active participants, learning to shape the dialogue that influences our every action and molds the reality we inhabit.

This book is structured to take you step by step through the intricate process of Mind Mirroring, a technique that reflects the essence of therapy and personal and spiritual development. Here is an overview of what each chapter entails:

Chapter 1: In this chapter, we will delve into how Mind Mirroring effectively replicates the therapeutic experience. It provides insight into how this technique serves as a self-guided form of therapy, enabling individuals to explore their inner world in a reflective and structured manner.

Chapter 2: We will explore the origins and principles of Gestalt therapy, focusing on its relationship with the empty chair technique. This chapter aims to provide a comprehensive background, helping you understand the foundations upon which Mind Mirroring is built. Understanding the nature of thought is crucial in the journey of self-awareness.

Chapter 3: We will delve into the nature of awareness and the dynamics of our thought processes, exploring how awareness of our thoughts can lead to profound self-insight and change.

Chapter 4: We will explore the meaning of responsibility as a singular, profound notion and an essential aspect of growth into higher consciousness.

Chapter 5: Here we will focus on the nature of personal and spiritual growth. This chapter will examine how Mind Mirroring not only facilitates personal development but also fosters spiritual growth, highlighting the interconnectedness of these two aspects of our being.

Chapter 6: We will explore the spiritual dimensions of Mind Mirroring and discuss how this practice can lead to deeper spiritual understanding and connection, reflecting on how our mental processes intersect with our spiritual lives.

Chapter 7: We will delve into the practical aspects of Mind Mirroring. This chapter provides a detailed guide on how to practice this simple technique, covering the essential 'nuts and bolts' to help you effectively engage in this transformative process.

Chapter 8: We will discuss how Mind Mirroring serves as a spontaneous improvisation of the mind. We will explore the dynamic and fluid nature of this practice, highlighting its capacity to mirror the improvisational aspect of human thought and emotion.

Chapter 9: In this chapter, we delve into the intricate process that characterizes human encounters illuminating the various elements that compose these interactions. This exploration serves as a foundation for understanding the self-reflective journey in Mind Mirroring, where the encounter takes an introspective turn, inviting you to a profound dialogue with yourself.

Chapter 10: As you practice Mind Mirroring, you are coming to know yourself as a mirror embodying all the qualities and functions of a mirror. Living your life as mirror is a profound concept that can have significant implications for how you perceive and interact with the world.

Chapter 11: We will offer some simple tips to creatively explore this process like practicing it on the fly and silently on the private stage of your mind.

Each chapter of "Mind Mirroring: The Magic of the Empty Chair" is designed to build upon the previous, creating a comprehensive guide that will support you on your journey of self-discovery and personal growth. Through this book, you will gain the tools and understanding necessary to engage deeply with your inner world and harness the transformative power of Mind Mirroring.

1. Embracing the Inner Therapist Through Mind Mirroring

"It is as if I am in the presence of a silent confidant who listens without judgment. The mirror chair becomes a silent partner in my journey of self-reflection, guiding me through the labyrinth of my own psyche, acknowledging every turn and echo of my inner voice."

What Brings People into Therapy?

In the pursuit of personal and spiritual growth, we often seek external guidance, looking for someone who will listen and understand us — a therapist. What drives anyone to see a therapist but "someone to talk to." There is some situation in life, some relationship, some emotion that we are not able to deal with on our own and so we search for a therapist who can listen and understand our inner state. Generally, we are not looking for the therapist to "fix" us, direct us, or give us any great words of wisdom but only to listen, empathize, and understand what we are experiencing. Things clear up just out of being heard and acknowledged for what we are feeling. The therapist need not perform great procedures that will somehow make us feel better. We feel better when another human being can truly "get" us.

But what if you could step into the role of being your own therapist? This is the transformative promise of Mind Mirroring, a practice that empowers you to bring the therapeutic conversation into the sanctuary of your own mind.

Just as in traditional therapy, Mind Mirroring invites you to bring forth your internal dialogues, feelings, concerns, and the narratives that shape your life. It is akin to sitting across from a therapist, except that the therapist is another aspect of you. The conversations you might typically reserve for the confidentiality of a therapy room are the ones you're invited to engage with here, using the Mind Mirroring technique.

When we seek therapy, we are often searching for a reflective surface — someone to listen deeply and reflect our words and feelings back to us. But how do we recognize when we've truly been heard by another? Sometimes, it's in the quality of the silence that follows our words, the nod that punctuates our sentences, the empathetic gaze that meets our own, or simply the words, "I hear you." Conversely, we know when we are not being heard. The other might have their own agenda or point of view about something that takes the conversation away from us. In our closest relationships, we all know the frustration when we are not being heard or when the other twists our words to an unintended meaning. Through Mind Mirroring, you will strive to listen to yourself accurately without an agenda. You will learn to give yourself the same level of acknowledgment and validation that a good therapist would.

A good therapist is someone who acts as a mirror reflecting back to us what we bring forth. In Mind Mirroring, you become the mirror, providing yourself with the undistorted reflection necessary for deep listening. The purpose is straightforward yet profound: to hear yourself with clarity and accuracy, to restore wholeness to your mind, and to achieve balance within your thought processes.

The Purpose of Therapy

The purpose of therapy is multifaceted, but at its core, it is about facilitating personal growth and healing. It aims to help individuals understand themselves better, cope with the challenges of life, make decisions, improve their relationships, and enhance their overall well-being.

Therapy seeks to change the way individuals experience their lives. This doesn't necessarily mean changing the external circumstances, but rather transforming the internal cognitive and emotional processes that dictate how one perceives and reacts to those circumstances.

Many people enter therapy to address specific psychological issues such as anxiety, depression, or the effects of trauma. The therapeutic process is designed to help them work through these issues, understand their origins, and develop healthier coping mechanisms.

Therapy often involves increasing self-awareness. By becoming more attuned to their emotions, thoughts, and behaviors, individuals can gain insight into their motivations and desires, which can lead to profound personal changes.

The statement "Learning to get out of my own way and allow life to unfold the way it does" refers to the idea of reducing resistance to life's natural course. This can involve letting go of the need to control every outcome, reducing the impact of past traumas on present behavior, and fostering an attitude of openness and acceptance.

Ultimately, therapy is about improving quality of life. This could mean finding more joy in everyday experiences, building richer and more fulfilling relationships, or feeling more engaged and purposeful in one's actions.

Therapy is a personal journey, and its purpose can vary widely among individuals. For some, it's about healing and recovery, while for others, it's about personal growth and self-actualization. The overarching goal is to support individuals in creating a life that feels more meaningful, satisfying, and joyful to them.

The Therapeutic Journey: Navigating the Terrain of Feelings

Therapy, at its core, is a journey through the landscape of our feelings. This journey begins at a point where we find ourselves feeling 'stuck' –

in a relationship, within our family dynamics, with memories of past events, in professional settings, or simply within our own thoughts and experiences. Often, it's a particular situation, past or ongoing, that serves as the catalyst for this sense of stagnation. Something happened or has been happening, leaving us feeling troubled, ensnared in a web of emotions and reactions that seem inescapable.

Feeling stuck can manifest in various forms – it might be a feeling of being trapped in a cycle of events or addictions, a persistent emotional state, or a series of reactions that seem beyond our control. These experiences are usually accompanied by a complex mix of emotions, many of which are uncomfortable or even painful. Guilt, anxiety, inadequacy, insecurity – these feelings often lead us to want to escape, to avoid confronting what we feel. This avoidance, however, often leads to acting out these emotions in ways that impact our happiness and well-being. Our lives, in this state, become dominated by the need to escape from these discomforting feelings, and ironically, from ourselves. This creates a circular pattern where change seems elusive, and the problems appear unresolvable.

This is where therapy transforms from an endeavor to 'fix' problems to a process of engaging with and understanding feelings. It's about acknowledging, accepting, and articulating these emotions. One of the most challenging aspects of therapy is finding the right words to describe what we feel, especially when some emotions seem indefinable. Yet, these unnamable feelings exert a profound influence on our peace of mind.

So, what does it mean to 'deal' with one's feelings in therapy? It's about facing them head-on. It involves feeling them fully, acknowledging their presence, articulating them, and taking ownership of them. Dealing with feelings also means confronting your thoughts and becoming a witness to the inner workings of your mind and emotional state.

In this light, therapy is not about fixing or changing anything in the conventional sense. It's about embracing what is there – the feelings, the thoughts, the emotions – and allowing them to be. In the therapeutic space, as you become a witness to your feelings, something remarkable happens. These troubling feelings and thoughts begin to dissolve, not because of any direct effort to change them, but simply by being acknowledged and observed. This process of witnessing allows emotions to flow and change naturally.

Thus, the essence of therapy lies in the paradox that by not actively trying to 'do' something about our feelings, we enable them to transform. This transformation is not a result of direct intervention, but a natural outcome of awareness and acceptance. In therapy, we learn that it's through the process of witnessing and acknowledging our inner landscape that we find the path to true change and healing. It's a journey not of escape, but of return – a return to a state of flow, where feelings and thoughts are neither suppressed nor acted out, but simply allowed to be, leading us towards a deeper understanding and acceptance of ourselves.

The Therapist's Primary Function

The therapist's primary function encompasses several key roles, each integral to the therapeutic process. This multifaceted approach is aimed at facilitating the client's journey toward self-understanding, healing, and growth.

The cornerstone of effective therapy is the therapist's ability to listen actively and accurately. This means fully engaging with the client's words, understanding the emotional undertones, and grasping the nuances of their communication. Active listening goes beyond simply hearing words; it involves a deep level of attentiveness and presence, ensuring the client feels heard and understood.

A therapist uses reflection as a tool to help clients gain insights into their thoughts and feelings. By mirroring back what the client has said, the therapist can help clarify and deepen the client's understanding of their own words. This reflection is not mere repetition; it involves synthesizing and sometimes paraphrasing the client's messages to highlight key themes and emotions.

Popularized by Carl Rogers, unconditional positive regard is a non-judgmental form of empathy and acceptance. It means accepting and respecting the client as they are, without imposing any conditions of worth. This attitude helps create a safe and supportive space where clients can explore their thoughts and feelings without fear of judgment or rejection.

Therapists often guide clients in a process of self-exploration, encouraging them to look inward to understand their emotions, thoughts, motivations, and behaviors. This process can involve asking probing questions that challenge clients to reflect deeply, helping them uncover underlying issues and gain self-awareness.

Focusing questions are used to guide the therapeutic conversation and to help clients concentrate on specific areas of their experience. These questions are designed to delve deeper into the client's psyche, uncovering layers of understanding and helping the client to see things from new perspectives.

Ultimately, the therapist's role is to facilitate the client's journey toward insight and self-discovery. This involves helping the client to connect the dots between past experiences and present behaviors, understand and manage emotions, and develop healthier coping mechanisms.

The therapist also works to establish a strong therapeutic alliance, which is the collaborative partnership between therapist and client. This relationship is based on trust, respect, and mutual understanding, and is crucial for effective therapy.

A significant function of the therapist is to empower the client. This means supporting the client in finding their own solutions and strengths, rather than providing direct advice or solutions. The aim is for clients to become more self-reliant and confident in their ability to handle life's challenges.

In summary, the therapist's primary function is multi-dimensional, encompassing active listening, reflection, unconditional positive regard, and focused inquiry, all aimed at facilitating a client's journey toward greater self-awareness, insight, and psychological well-being. This process is not about directing or dictating the client's path, but rather supporting and guiding them as they navigate their own journey of growth and healing.

The Essence of Reflection as Awareness and the Divine

Reflection, in its purest essence, is an act of awareness, a fundamental attribute that mirrors the entirety of existence. Envision a mirror—its fundamental function is to reflect without alteration or delay. It does not discriminate, alter, or offer directives; it simply presents a direct image of whatever stands before it. This act of reflection is not just a property of physical mirrors but is also intrinsic to the nature of consciousness and, in a broader, more spiritual sense, to the divine.

Consider the inherent qualities of a mirror: It portrays things precisely as they are. When we peer into it, our image gazes back with immediacy, capturing us in our true form. There is no judgment emanating from the mirror, no critique—it reflects our essence in the moment. If discontent arises from our reflection, it is not the mirror that casts aspersions; rather, it is our own perceptions and judgments that color what we see. The mirror is impartial, reflecting back to us not only our image but our reactions to it.

When we desire a different reflection, it is not the mirror we must alter but ourselves. The mirror is swift to show the change, illustrating that transformation is a direct consequence of our own actions. It does not resist; it perpetually accepts and reveals our present state. In a similar vein, when love and acceptance are what we present, they are immediately reflected back to us.

The mirror metaphor extends to the divine, wherein the divine is likened to an ultimate mirror, eternally reflecting the reality of our being. It does not matter what actions we undertake; this divine reflection is constant, offering acceptance without condition. The mirror of existence is not confined to a specific place or time; it is omnipresent, found in the here and now. It underscores the unity between the observer and the observed, blurring the lines between self and reflection, signifying oneness.

When we gaze outward into the world, we are, in effect, gazing into a vast, cosmic mirror—every aspect of our environment reflects a part of us back to ourselves. We are not merely observers of the universe; we are integrally woven into its fabric, indivisible from the whole. This realization dawns through awareness, which allows us to observe our existence as a mirror does: with clarity, immediacy, and without judgment.

Awareness, then, is not an entity or a tangible thing; it transcends physicality while encompassing all that is. It serves as the sacred platform from which we witness the unfolding of life. If we view life as a grand play of separation from the divine, then awareness is the cosmic stage upon which we come to recognize our true unity with the divine and with all creation. Awareness is the very essence of presence, omnipresent in every moment, embodying the divine presence in all.

In contemplating this, we come to see that the immediate change, the 'twinkling of an eye' transformation, is not a protracted journey but an instantaneous shift in perception—a recognition of our constant, unbroken connection to the divine, mirrored back to us in every facet of our being and existence.

2. Background of Gestalt Therapy and the Two-Chair Process

<hr>

"Engaging with the mind mirroring exercise, I've come to understand that if there is something to be gleaned, it's the practice of living firmly within the moment. This exercise cultivates a life centered in reality—a reality that's embraced through the lens of love and acceptance. It's a method that unveils the myriad of thoughts that often obstruct this state of awareness."

Gestalt therapy provides the foundation of the two-chair process which is the hallmark of the Mind Mirroring technique. Gestalt therapy is an existential and experiential form of psychotherapy that emphasizes personal responsibility and focuses on the individual's experience in the present moment. It is a holistic approach that regards the individual as a complete being rather than a collection of symptoms or behaviors to be corrected. Developed by Fritz Perls in the 1940s and 1950s, Gestalt therapy arose as a reaction to the predominance of analytic and behaviorist psychology, offering a more immediate, embodied, and relational approach to psychological healing and growth.

Psychodrama: Merging Drama with Psychology

Gestalt psychology traces its origins back to the early 1920s with its prominence primarily confined to Germany. On the global stage, the limelight was on Freud, Jung, and Adler, with the training of psychotherapists and psychiatrists often rooted in their philosophies. In contrast, Gestalt was grounded in neuro-physiological experiments intertwined with mathematical and physical principles. Gestalt psychology could be aptly termed, the "psychology of wholeness" where behavior and internal processes could best be understood in terms of the laws of wholeness, where figure and background form the whole of experience.

Gestalt psychology rapidly became a frontrunner in Germany. However, its global recognition was limited, with familiarity often restricted to those who pursued postgraduate studies in Berlin or Munich. With the rise of Hitler, many of the forerunners in Gestalt psychology fled to America where they continued to articulate the nature of human behavior and experience from the laws of wholeness.

Gestalt therapy traces its roots to a psychiatrist named Jacob Moreno, who became versed in Gestalt Psychology. Moreno, having qualifications in both medicine and psychiatry discerned the value of the Gestalt approach. Due to his inclination towards theater and a lineage rooted in the dramatic arts, Moreno realized that theatrical performances essentially replicated real-life situations. Within these staged environments, actors must momentarily shed their personal identities and emotions. They had to adopt a new persona, seeing the world through an entirely different lens, and reacting based on the character's psyche.

This continual shift in roles, transitioning from one character to another—imbued actors with exceptional adaptability, consciously reshaping their personalities by creative choice. Recognizing this transformative potential, Moreno incorporated this theatrical methodology into his psychiatric practice, giving birth to the global movement known as psychodrama. Moreno saw psychodrama as the next logical step beyond psychoanalysis. It was an opportunity to get into action instead of just talking, to take the role of the important people in our lives to understand them better, to confront them imaginatively in the safety of the therapeutic theater, and most of all to become more creative and spontaneous human beings.

Globalizing his vision, Moreno founded psychiatric clinics worldwide. His own kin were trained to participate in these therapeutic enactments.

He also trained directors, usually from psychiatry or clinical psychology backgrounds, to oversee these dramatized therapy sessions. Moreno's method was distinctive: instead of attempting to modify an individual's behavior to fit a specific situation, he crafted an entirely new scenario that resonated with the individual's behavior. When participants acted in such tailored settings, there was a synchronicity between their internal feelings and the external staged reality.

Considering that psychological conflicts arise from a misalignment between an individual's internal sentiments and their external circumstances, this approach had a profound therapeutic impact. Participants, once they truly embraced these constructed settings, began to identify the origins of their behaviors. Within these artificially designed situations, their actions became perfectly coherent, even to outsiders. Moreno demonstrated that every situation in life can be likened to a theatrical performance.

While Moreno penned numerous texts elaborating on these concepts, the implementation of psychodrama required someone with a holistic understanding of Gestalt psychology coupled with theatrical prowess. Only a highly creative and intuitive person could genuinely harness its therapeutic potential. Sadly, many psychodramatic practices devolved into mere theatrical displays, lacking the foundational ethos Moreno had envisioned.

As Perls' commitment to psychoanalysis started to wane, he delved deep into Gestalt psychology, studying Moreno's psychodrama. Fritz envisioned extracting the dramatic essence of psychodrama to formulate a direct therapeutic technique employing an empty chair situated directly in front of the person, eliminating the need for an elaborate staged setup.

His innovative approach involved patients enacting various facets of their issues, making them their own actors within self-created scenarios.

This therapeutic technique became Fritz's signature method once he resumed his practice in California. Around this time, he interacted with prominent figures in the human potential movement, such as Maslow and Carl Rogers. Many, seeing the efficacy of his methods, became his pupils.

Fritz's therapy sessions transformed into spectacles. In workshops, he'd engage with individuals before large audiences, inviting them on stage to dissect and address their challenges. The electric atmosphere led to attendees eagerly participating, revealing their deepest troubles. Fritz's groundbreaking approach didn't just gain him personal acclaim; it also reshaped psychiatric practices across America, with Gestalt Therapy influencing nearly two-thirds of all psychiatric work in the country.

Perl's Innovative Approach: The Two-Chair Process and Dreamwork

Fritz Perls' groundbreaking contributions to Gestalt therapy include the innovative two-chair process and a unique approach to dreamwork. These techniques revolutionized the understanding and treatment of internal conflicts and unconscious communication.

The two-chair technique, a cornerstone of Perls' methodology, involves an individual engaging in a physical dialogue between conflicting aspects of their consciousness. By physically moving between two chairs, the individual embodies each side of the conflict, fostering communication and awareness within themselves. This process allows for the externalization and reconciliation of internal disputes, offering a tangible space for confrontation and resolution. It encourages clients to explore different facets of their personality or internalized dialogues, often leading to significant breakthroughs in self-understanding and emotional release. The technique helps in assimilating suppressed or denied parts, thereby aiding in achieving a unified sense of self.

Perls' approach to dreamwork marked a departure from traditional symbolic interpretation methods. He encouraged individuals to 'become' each symbol in their dream, embodying and expressing it to uncover the dream's meaning through experiential identification. This method views dreams as internal psychodramas, communicative acts from one part of the person to another, occurring during sleep when the verbal faculty is dormant, but the symbolic, imaging part remains active. This form of communication relies on imagery rather than sound, linking the conscious and unconscious mind.

In Gestalt dreamwork, emotions connected to these images act as bridges, linking conscious experiences with symbolic imagery. Perls believed these symbols were projections or disowned parts of the self. The objective of dreamwork is to 're-own' these aspects and integrate them into one's full personality, promoting a sense of wholeness. The therapist, acting as a director, suggests that clients 'become' various objects from their dream, describing themselves as these objects. This process transcends strict symbolic interpretation, focusing on completion and integration through identification.

Both the two-chair technique and dreamwork in Gestalt therapy emphasize self-awareness and integration. By enacting dialogues, either with different parts of the dream or between conflicting internal perceptions, individuals gain deep insights into their own feelings and thoughts. This experiential learning aids in assimilating various aspects of the self, often leading to profound emotional catharsis and personal growth.

The two-chair technique particularly makes abstract internal conflicts concrete, providing a literal space for individuals to confront and work through their issues. This method aligns with the Gestalt therapy goals of achieving present-centered awareness, self-acceptance, and holistic personal development.

In conclusion, Perls' methods in Gestalt therapy, including the two-chair process and dreamwork, offer powerful tools for individuals to explore and integrate various aspects of their psyche. These techniques foster a deeper understanding of oneself and facilitate a journey toward a more unified and authentic self.

Core Principles of Gestalt Therapy

Gestalt therapy places emphasis on the present moment, the "here and now." It encourages clients to fully experience the present rather than dwell on narratives of the past or worry about the future. Therapists assist clients in becoming more aware of what they are doing in the moment, what they are feeling, and how they are experiencing themselves at this moment in relationship to others and to past events. Change naturally occurs simply out of being present, and exploring their present experience, while learning to accept and value themselves.

A central tenet of Gestalt therapy is the cultivation of awareness. Awareness is observing one's thoughts, feelings, behaviors, bodily sensations, and the surrounding environment in the here and now. The therapy sessions are an exploration aimed at enhancing the client's self-awareness and mindfulness in their daily life.

Gestalt therapy is founded on the principle of wholeness, perceiving each individual as a holistic composition of thoughts, emotions, physicality, and spirituality. At its core is the figure/ground principle, pivotal in Gestalt psychology. This principle underscores that the most salient aspects of an individual's experience, referred to as 'figural', are the immediate and dominant emotions. These emotions are often intricately linked to unresolved or 'ground' issues from one's past. The primary objective of Gestalt therapy is to guide clients in addressing and resolving these unresolved past experiences, thereby facilitating a journey toward comprehensive self-awareness and self-acceptance.

Central to this therapeutic process is the encouragement of clients to recognize responsibility for their feelings, actions, choices, and their role in shaping their life circumstances. This approach empowers individuals, instilling a sense of agency and control over their life's direction. Gestalt therapy posits that emotions from past unresolved experiences can persist and impact one's current functioning. The therapy focuses on bringing these lingering "unfinished" feelings into the conscious present, allowing them to be fully experienced, processed, and ultimately resolved. Through this process, clients can achieve a state of emotional clarity and well-being, aligning their present experience with their intrinsic wholeness.

The term 'contact' refers to the way in which individuals interact with their environment and encounters with others. Gestalt therapy explores the quality of these interactions and how they may be impeded by psychological and emotional blockages. The therapeutic relationship itself becomes a microcosm for examining and resolving issues related to the quality of contact with others.

Gestalt therapy is well-known for its creative and experimental techniques, such as role-play, the empty chair technique, and guided fantasy, to name a few. These methods are used to explore clients' feelings, test out new ways of thinking and behaving, and move beyond their habitual patterns.

The paradox of change in Gestalt therapy proposes that individuals change most effectively when they stop trying to be something they are not and instead become more fully who they are. When clients focus on what they are experiencing in the present, change occurs naturally as a byproduct of increased insight and self-awareness.

The practice of Gestalt therapy can be deeply transformative, moving clients toward self-recognition and acceptance, enabling them to navigate their lives with a greater sense of freedom and authenticity.

Mind Mirroring as an Embodiment of Gestalt Therapy

Mind Mirroring, as a reflective therapeutic technique, beautifully encapsulates the core principles of Gestalt therapy, creating a unique tapestry that weaves together personal growth with the thread of Gestalt philosophy.

At the heart of Mind Mirroring lies the commitment to the present moment. By engaging in this technique, individuals are not just recalling past scenes or anticipating future responses; they are fully immersed in the current act of expression and reflection. This practice anchors them in the 'here and now,' which is a foundational aspect of Gestalt therapy, allowing for a direct and immediate encounter with their own thoughts and feelings.

Mind Mirroring elevates self-awareness. The speaker chair invites candid self-expression, while the mirror chair offers a unique opportunity to hear one's own words echoed back without embellishment. This mirroring effect magnifies the consciousness of one's internal state, making the individual acutely aware of their habitual patterns of thought and emotional responses.

By acknowledging and reflecting the totality of what the speaker communicates, Mind Mirroring fosters a sense of completeness. Participants are encouraged to embrace and speak all parts of themselves that emerge in the moment — the rational, the emotional, the physical, and the spiritual. Through this technique, the fragmented aspects of the self are brought into a harmonious whole, honoring Gestalt's principle of integration.

In the speaker's chair, individuals own their narrative; in the mirror chair, they own their reflections. Mind Mirroring promotes a personal responsibility for one's words and reactions. There is no external analyst providing interpretation — the individual is the creator and observer of their own experience, emphasizing the Gestalt ethos of self-responsibility.

The mirror chair can become a vessel for the expression of unprocessed emotions and unresolved past experiences. As individuals reflect on their spoken words, they are able to recognize and address their unfinished business. This reflection provides a path to closure, allowing them to engage with these emotions in the present, which is essential for Gestalt therapeutic work.

Mind Mirroring enriches the contact between the self and the mirrored self, enhancing the relationship an individual has with their own inner being. It mirrors the Gestalt emphasis on how we engage with ourselves and the world around us, highlighting potential disruptions in this relationship and providing a clear space for exploration and healing.

Gestalt therapy is known for its creative and experiential approaches, and Mind Mirroring fits this mold by providing an innovative way to experiment with self-perception and self-dialogue. It allows individuals to try new ways of relating to themselves and their internal narratives in a safe, controlled environment.

Through Mind Mirroring, change is facilitated by the act of becoming more of what one already is, rather than striving to change oneself into something they are not. This is the paradox of change operating in the here and now. By reflecting the self back to the self, individuals are invited to meet themselves as they are. When we give up trying to change and turn that attempt into full awareness and acceptance, this creates the fertile ground for natural and spontaneous change — a core belief of Gestalt therapy.

Mind Mirroring, therefore, is not just an exercise in self-reflection; it is a living embodiment of Gestalt therapy principles, offering a pathway to deeper self-knowledge and transformation. It provides a structured yet flexible framework that supports the Gestalt therapeutic process, leading to heightened self-awareness, integration, and authenticity.

3. Awareness

"Engaging with the mind mirroring exercise, I've come to understand that if there is something to be gleaned, it's the practice of living firmly within the moment. This exercise cultivates a life centered in reality—a reality that's embraced through the lens of love and acceptance. It's a method that unveils the myriad of thoughts that often obstruct this state of awareness."

While "awareness" may be a noun, symbolizing the backdrop of existence, the act "to be aware" suggests an ongoing engagement with the present. Being aware beckons you to attentively embrace the immediate reality of your existence. This moment, as you are reading these words, in this very place, you are experiencing something in your body and thinking something. This is your present action that is unfolding just as it is, moving toward completion and transitioning into the next action. This is the essence of the cycles of your life from birth to death.

Awareness invites you to continually inquire...

"What am I doing right now, in this place, and what am I experiencing right now within this vessel of being?"

This questioning is pivotal to the idea of awareness and the Mind Mirroring process.

We thus delineate awareness as the fresh observation of each unfolding moment, *as it is*. The pivotal elements of this understanding are 'observation' and 'experiencing.' Observation is confined to the present, the 'now,' and is bound to the 'here.' Since neither past nor future hold tangibility, they elude observation. The bygone is irretrievable, the yet-to-come remains concealed. Observability is also limited to that which falls within the purview of the senses. Your current locale, as you assimilate these words, constitutes the sole sphere observable by you.

Within the spectrum of any instant, there exist three realms of awareness or observation, within which your existence is experienced.

First is the realm of the external world: comprising objects, entities, individuals, circumstances, and events within your immediate vicinity. Each scenario bears unique attributes, and by virtue of your presence, you become an integral part of every context. Your actions and interactions with the people and objects around you shape your experiences in relation to your environment. You engage with the chair you are sitting on, with the device delivering these words to you, with the myriad objects surrounding you, the atmosphere, and the energy in your space.

Next is the realm of the internal world encompassing bodily sensations and movements. At this moment, you are experiencing sensations within your body and enacting movements, however subtle they may be. You may not be aware of these sensations in this present moment, but they are there, available for you to observe.

Lastly is the realm of the mind: filled with language and imagery. Presently, your mind is engaged in the articulation of thoughts and the visualization of images.

Your life unfurls within these three domains, and you possess the faculty to witness the activities occurring within your present experience. Countless phenomena in this instant escape your notice, and as you engage your awareness, a richer understanding of both your personal reality and the broader tapestry of life begins to unfold.

As you absorb these words, take a moment to leisurely rotate your head, allowing your gaze to sweep across your immediate surroundings. Note the diversity of objects entering your field of vision, briefly acknowledging each before your awareness settles on a single item.

Observe its form, tracing the contours with your eyes, and notice how, in this focused state, all else fades into the background. Observe the hues it presents...

In this brief span, you are engaged in observation. If you prolonged your focus, the object would reveal further intricacies.

Now, shift to the auditory. Tune in to the sounds permeating your space. Discern their proximity and rhythm, isolating one from the mix. As your attention narrows, other sounds dim...

Here, you are observing auditory phenomena. Prolonged attention might unveil sounds previously unnoticed, highlighting the depth of your environment.

Draw your awareness closer, to your body's posture. Sense your limbs' arrangement, feel the subtleties of movement, the pressure where your body meets the chair, and observe your breath's ebb and flow. Can you detect the pulse of your heart?

In doing so, you observe bodily sensations that, until prompted, eluded your consciousness.

Turning to the domain of the mind, consider the myriad thoughts coursing unseen. If you focus, you'll find your mind flitting from thoughts of duty to memories, anticipations, judgments, fleeting musings—a cavalcade of mental activity.

Take a moment to step back, eyes closed, and watch this mental parade. Listen for the internal dialogue, witness the imagery. Attempt to "catch" a thought...

Observing the mind is a subtle art, foundational to meditation, challenging due to the immersive nature of thought. Living within your mind obscures its landscape from view.

Step back. You'll realize you're in constant self-dialogue, bombarded by past reflections and future projections, often outside conscious realization. Awareness and meditation strive to illuminate this ceaseless inner discourse.

In every moment, you're enmeshed in these domains of awareness: the external world, bodily sensations, and the mental arena. They coalesce into a comprehensive experience, revealing your totality, your Self. These domains are not separate but a seamless whole. The challenge lies in not getting ensnared by thought, which disrupts the continuity of awareness. To maintain the flow is to sustain awareness, embodying the unity of your experience.

The Landscape of the Mind: Words and Pictures

Our mind is a canvas where words and images continuously represent the narrative of our thoughts. This intricate tapestry of mental activity encompasses everything from simple notions to complex imaginations. Essentially, all these diverse elements can be encapsulated under the broad term 'thought'. We engage in thought through a duality of language - the words we 'hear' internally and the pictures we 'see' within our mind's eye.

When we delve into the past, these mental images are known as memories. Recollecting a past event is akin to visualizing a scene or episode in our mind. These memory flashes might be brief or enduring, often becoming a preoccupation, especially if the memory is of a disturbing nature. We might replay these memories repeatedly, experiencing them as still or moving images, which can dominate our mental landscape.

Conversely, when we cast our thoughts toward the future, the mental pictures take the form of expectations, anticipations, or visions. Planning or contemplating future actions involves 'seeing' these events unfold in our imagination. These future-oriented images guide our actions and intentions. Whether it's expecting something from someone or envisioning a forthcoming event, these images are previews of potential future realities.

Our mind's eye also conjures images of people, scenarios, and fantasies. These might include fond or unfavorable images of others, daydreams about winning the lottery or imagining different life situations. It's crucial to recognize that these images are not reality; they are fabrications of our mind. By acknowledging these images in the present moment, we anchor ourselves back in reality, understanding that past and future are merely constructs of the mind manifesting in the now.

Thoughts often manifest as subvocal words, forming an internal dialogue on the mind's private stage. This dialogue can include statements, questions, commands, and exclamations. We find ourselves constantly engaged in this inner conversation, sometimes with ourselves, other times with imagined others. These mental sentences might be remnants of past experiences or rehearsals for future encounters. They can express different facets of our personality, some of which we're acutely aware of, and others that remain in our subconscious. Often, we become so immersed in these internal dialogues that they begin to dictate our actions and emotions.

The spectrum of thought is vast and varied. It ranges from abstract thinking, which involves generalization and conceptualization, to concrete thinking focused on immediate, tangible objects. Some minds wander through mathematical equations and relationships, while others may hear melodies and musical notes.

In summary, the mind is a dynamic, ever-evolving theater of words and pictures – a realm where memories, anticipations, fantasies, and internal dialogues converge to create our unique mental landscape. Understanding and navigating this landscape is key to gaining insight into our behavior, emotions, and overall perception of the world around us.

The Experience of Imaging and Self-Talk

In the intricate dance of our inner world, 'imaging' and 'self-talk' are the fundamental components from which all types of thoughts spring. These elements form the scaffold for our beliefs and feelings, shaping our perceptions and experiences. When we engage in this mental activity unconsciously, it can lead to a range of human problems, from anxiety and depression to conflicts in our relationships. Recognizing and understanding this process is key to gaining control over our mental landscape.

At the heart of our mental process lies the act of creating thoughts. Thoughts do not simply appear; they are crafted by our creative imagination and internal narratives. This realization empowers us with the understanding that we are the architects of our thoughts. We create our reality through the thoughts we choose to entertain and the beliefs we decide to hold. This realization is crucial in understanding that we are not passive recipients of thoughts but active participants in their formation.

Being present to our inner processes involves a conscious engagement with our thoughts and feelings. Often, we might find ourselves avoiding uncomfortable thoughts or feelings, a tendency that underpins many addictive behaviors. Addressing an addiction, therefore, involves confronting and expressing these feelings rather than seeking escape through substances or behaviors. Articulating our feelings accurately can be challenging but is essential for true understanding and healing.

Thoughts and feelings are inextricably linked – they are two facets of the same experience. When we undergo a crisis, for instance, it's not just the external events that impact us but also the internal tumult of thoughts and feelings. One of the aims of awareness practices like Mind Mirroring is to articulate these experiences, distinguishing between thoughts and feelings. This process brings us into the present, helping us to understand and express what we are experiencing now.

Speaking our present experience involves more than recounting past events; it's about delving into what we are experiencing in the here and now in relationship to these events. The purpose of sharing our story is to understand the background of our present experiences. This is the gestalt figure/ground in operation. What is 'figural' are the present feelings and what is 'ground' is the story or recounting of a troubling situation.

All persistent feelings have their origin in past events. The idea in therapy is to explore and finish these feelings. This exploration begins with the question, *"What am I experiencing right now?"* Answering this question requires honesty and spontaneity. We complete the sentence *"Right now, I am experiencing..."* with whatever feels true in this moment, even if there is a lack of immediate clarity. This practice highlights our role as observers and explorers of our experiences, shaped by the words we choose to use.

While thoughts themselves are silent, we give them voice through our choice of words. Whether it's verbalizing a current thought as *"Right now, I am thinking..."* or describing an image in our mind, *"Right now I am imagining..."* we are actively translating our silent thoughts and images into spoken or written words. This verbalization *represents* our thoughts, but they are not the thoughts themselves. No one can know what we think or feel unless we communicate. We are the sole experiencer of our experience.

As we engage with the world around us, our mind continually processes a stream of words and images. This flow is constant, whether we are silently reading, meditating, or actively speaking. Understanding this flow helps us realize that we have the power to shape our experiences through the words we choose, the thoughts we entertain, and the beliefs we nurture.

In summary, 'imaging' and 'self-talk' are powerful elements that shape our mental landscape. By becoming aware of and actively engaging with these processes, we can transform our inner dialogue, leading to a more conscious and fulfilling life. This chapter underscores the importance of being present to our thoughts and feelings, recognizing our role in creating and observing them, and understanding the profound impact they have on our overall well-being.

Communicating Awareness of Thought

In the intricate dance of human interaction and self-expression, our understanding and communication of thoughts and feelings play a crucial role. Often, we are not fully conscious of our thoughts as distinct entities. When we say, *"I think...",* we tend to *become* the thought itself, losing our identity to it. This conflation is a fundamental error, as it equates our entire being with mere thoughts. You are not just your thoughts; you *have* thoughts, but they are not the entirety of who you are.

Recognizing a thought as just a thought requires verbalizing awareness. When you say, *"Right now I am aware of thinking...",* you are effectively naming and describing a thought in the here and now. This process is about using words to articulate other words. Similarly, saying, *"Right now I am aware of picturing..."* uses words to describe an image. This is a form of meta-communication – communicating from a place of awareness. The essence of understanding thought lies in the ability to communicate your thoughts as distinct from your being.

Communication in relationships often transcends the mere exchange of stories or information. While these are aspects of everyday interaction, they often overlook the immediacy of the present moment's experience. Most traditional communication revolves around past events or future plans, ideas, or concepts, rarely focusing on what is happening in the here and now, where the entirety of life unfolds. In short, we get lost in the labyrinth of thoughts of past and future.

True communication is structured; it involves the 'I' of awareness and the object of observation within the context of an encounter with 'you'. Presence becomes more tangible as a 'you' becomes present in the conversation. True communication isn't just talking *about* something unless it's consciously shared as such. It's about *being* something in the moment, sharing your presence with another which is beyond words. Sharing your present experience involves observing your thoughts and feelings as they occur and then verbalizing this awareness with another.

Relationships are fundamentally about relating. This process is reciprocal, involving a sequence of expression and response where two individuals reveal their awareness to each other. In this encounter, the experience of oneness becomes a lived reality, merging 'I' and 'You' into 'We'.

Communication isn't always verbal. In fact, we are constantly communicating with the world around us. It's impossible not to communicate, as being itself is a form of communication. Whether it's with objects, animals, or people, communication occurs. The challenge in each encounter is to articulate the non-verbal communication that emerges. Often, the words we use do not reflect our true experience, leading to inauthentic communication. Authentic communication, where words match experience, is rare but deeply impactful.

Thoughts, feelings, memories, and body sensations emerge in encounters with others. True communication arises when we allow curiosity about these experiences and share them. Sharing experiences is both the art and risk of relating, opening avenues for genuine connection and understanding.

In essence, communicating awareness of thought is about recognizing and articulating thoughts as distinct entities from our being. It involves a conscious effort to engage in authentic communication, where we share not just information, but our real-time experiences and existence with others. Mind Mirroring activates our awareness of thought thereby enriching our relationships, making them more meaningful and deeply connected.

4. Responsibility

―――

"Engaging with the Mind Mirroring technique has become a profound aspect of my daily life. It's as if the practice has opened a door to a new dimension of consciousness. Now, I find myself seamlessly integrating the technique into my everyday moments—while alone, I'll often catch myself in real-time, reflecting on my spontaneous inner dialogues. Even amidst company, I sometimes engage in this reflective practice silently."

The concept of responsibility is multifaceted, carrying different implications in various contexts. One common interpretation associates responsibility with fault or blame, particularly in situations where something has gone wrong. Another perspective views responsibility as a trait of reliability and dependability, such as in the context of financial obligations or personal character. In a professional setting, being 'responsible' might refer to holding a position of authority or accountability. Additionally, responsibility can denote a guardianship role, like a parent's duty towards their child.

However, when we shift to the realm of personal experience, the meaning of responsibility simplifies to a singular, profound notion:

"I am the creator of my experience. I am creating my experience just as it is and how I would have it be."

This understanding is anchored in innocence and personal power. It eschews blame and fault-finding, instead recognizing the individual as a powerful creator, often in denial of their own capacity. Denying responsibility for one's existence often leads to a victim mentality, where life's events seem to occur arbitrarily, rendering the individual powerless and helpless.

The mirror analogy offers a clear illustration of this concept. Just as a mirror simply reflects without judgment or alteration, everything we experience in life is a reflection of our own doing. The mirror doesn't inflict punishment or pass judgment; it reflects unconditionally, without malice or favor.

The statement *"I am responsible for what I see in the mirror"* encapsulates a deep psychological truth, emphasizing the role of personal accountability in how we perceive and interpret our own reflections—both literal and metaphorical. In the context of self-reflection and personal growth, this phrase suggests that individuals hold the power to shape their self-perception, attitudes, and reactions to their internal experiences.

When we engage in practices like Mind Mirroring, we're not just passive observers but active participants in a dialogue with ourselves. The "mirror" serves as a metaphor for the feedback we receive from our own thoughts and feelings. By acknowledging responsibility for this internal feedback, we recognize that our self-talk, judgments, and criticisms are products of our own creation. This is empowering because it implies that we can transform these patterns through conscious effort.

Taking responsibility for what appears in the mirror means we cannot blame others for our internal state; we own our emotions, biases, and projections. It's a call to self-awareness, urging us to examine how our inner critic might distort what we see, how our past experiences shape our current worldview, and how we might be perpetuating negative self-concepts.

The phrase also implies that we have the power to change the narrative. Just as we can choose to shift our focus from flaws to strengths in a physical mirror, we can choose to redirect our mental and emotional energy toward compassion, understanding, and acceptance through our psychological mirror. Recognizing that we are responsible for what we see is the first step toward transforming our self-perception and, by extension, our reality.

Grasping the idea that one is responsible for their own existence is a pivotal realization. It means acknowledging oneself as the creator of their life's experiences. The ego mind may resist this notion fiercely, persistently maintaining a narrative of helplessness, unfairness, and victimhood. This ego-driven voice is insistent, painting oneself as a puppet to circumstances, inherently flawed or guilty.

Yet, the truth lies beyond this illusion. You are not inherently bad, guilty, or wrong. Such self-condemning beliefs are the ego's desperate attempts to maintain its narrative. Every action deemed wrong or bad is instantly corrected in the grand scheme of existence. Mistakes and errors in judgment are a part of life, but they do not define your worth or fate.

You have the power to step out of this self-imposed prison of guilt and negative beliefs. The key to this prison is within your grasp – it is your thoughts and beliefs that lock you in. Recognizing this fact is akin to realizing the prison door has always been open. You can choose to walk out, leaving behind the shackles of self-imposed limitations and delusions.

In essence, responsibility in the context of awareness is about acknowledging and embracing your role as the creator of your experiences. It's about stepping out of the victim mindset and recognizing that you have the power to shape your reality. This realization is liberating, allowing you to live a life of conscious choice rather than one dictated by unconscious beliefs and patterns.

Responsibility in the Context of Relationships

In your existence as a human, you are immersed in a complex vibrational field, interconnected in a vast web of relationships with everyone and everything around you. Your life is a constant interplay of these vibrational influences – you receive them from others' thoughts, beliefs, emotions, and actions, and you also contribute your own vibrations to this collective field.

To transcend beyond mere existence and actively engage with the universe, a profound acceptance is required. This acceptance is encapsulated in the realization:

"I accept all experiences that enter my awareness, taking full responsibility for my moment-to-moment experiences. I acknowledge myself as the creator of my experience and take responsibility for the meanings I assign to these experiences."

This acknowledgment fundamentally alters your perception of life. It eradicates the notion of being a victim to unseen forces or external circumstances. You can no longer fault others or project blame; you recognize the futility of judgment within your conscious mind; and you come to see that the past does not determine the present. This realization is pivotal for those who seek to awaken fully and embrace their true essence.

You have the freedom to accept or reject this perspective. Clinging to victimhood, perceiving events as inherently good or bad, or believing that things happen to you independent of your interpretations, keeps you shackled in a state of illusion. By choosing to see yourself as a victim, you trap yourself in a cycle of weakness, fear, self-doubt, and separation from the divine essence.

Awareness is your inherent state of being. Through choiceless awareness, you experience life fully, determining how you interact with what you attract into your life. These experiences do not define you; you are the awareness, the space in which all experiences manifest.

In this state of awareness, you are akin to a wave, filled with the same immense power as the ocean. You have the freedom to choose which vibrations to integrate into your being, which thoughts to defend, and which perceptions to attach to yourself. Surrendering to your existence means giving up resistance to your life, embracing it fully, and deciding to thrive in the vitality of your being, eternal and boundless.

You are not a victim of your perceived world; you are a ceaseless creator, sharing the essence with the Creator. The challenge lies in recognizing that you are not merely the creations you observe; you are the creator. Knowing yourself as the creator empowers you to use your awareness deliberately, choosing the vibrations and relationships you allow into your life.

Your potential is limitless. The thoughts and perceptions you choose will resonate throughout your life, shaping your experiences, even the transition we call death. By thinking only with a mind aligned with the divine – thinking lovingly, infinitely, timelessly, and playfully – you tap into the true essence of existence. This approach lets you experience love and joy so profound that it overflows, compelling you to share this energy with all of creation.

In summary, living in the vibrational field of relationships means embracing the role of a conscious creator. It's about realizing that your thoughts and perceptions shape your reality, and by changing these, you can transform your experiences. This chapter calls for a shift from a mindset of victimhood to one of empowered creation, where every thought and feeling is an opportunity to shape your journey through life and beyond.

Responsibility for Guilt and Fear

As a being intricately connected to a vast web of relationships and experiences, your primary obstacle to fully embracing your role as a creator is guilt and fear. Guilt and fear are two polarities of living in the past and future, with guilt arising from past actions and fear arising from anticipated negative outcomes. Mastering creation involves learning to dissolve these persistent feelings in all their manifestations with resentments, shame, and regret as elements of guilt, and worry, anxiety, self-doubt, and apprehension, as elements of fear. The key to dissolving guilt and fear is not in resisting or hating these feelings, but in observing them with perfect innocence, embracing and studying them as a scientist would study a phenomenon.

When confronted with guilt or fear, you can adopt a stance of curiosity and innocence through self-inquiry:

With guilt, you can ask, *"What exactly do I feel guilty about and what are my guilty thoughts?"* then fill in the blank a series of times with this phrase, *"I feel guilty about... and my guilty thoughts are..."*

With fear you can ask, *"What exactly am I afraid of, and how do I experience this fear in my body?"* then fill in the blank with this phrase, *"I'm afraid of... and I feel... in my body."*

By closely unconcealing and revealing our guilts and fears, we start to break them up, preventing them from becoming permanent fixtures in our consciousness. You come to realize that guilt and fear is a function of the *words you say* and the *images you create* on the private stage of your mind. Reflect on different areas of your life and relationships and bring these questions into self-examination and answer them for yourself. Acknowledge both the small and significant guilts and fears that arise.

Mastery in life is about embracing yourself as a ceaseless creator, taking complete responsibility for all that enters your field of awareness without judgment. This stance allows you to decide whether to retain or dissolve these experiences. Living fearlessly means no longer fearing the infinite, creative power that comes from your perfect union with the divine. As Jesus said, *"I and my Father are one,"* he implied the same unity for all – you are one with God, and so is everyone else.

Every moment, you are actively using your unlimited power to create. You remain free to create anew at any time. What you experience in the future is the direct result of the thoughts you choose to entertain now.

The pivotal question then becomes...

"Am I, as a being created in the image of God, willing to consciously and actively choose to be responsible for the thoughts I allow into my mind each moment?"

The ultimate choice lies in deciding between clinging to old patterns of blame and victimhood, or embracing the joy and freedom of creation. The question, *"Would I rather be right or be happy?"* serves as a reminder that true happiness and fulfillment lie in acknowledging your creative power and taking responsibility for your experiences.

Love is the mirror image of awareness, both accepting all unconditionally. Your true self is grounded in awareness, and since awareness equates to love, your fundamental essence is love—whole, complete, and boundless.

With Mind Mirroring, you are activating your awareness of 'what is' in your consciousness and verbalizing that awareness, allowing the mirror to reflect this back. You become the mirror of your existence and not the thoughts you think.

In summary, moving beyond guilt and fear and embracing your role as a creator requires a shift in perspective. It involves observing these feelings understanding your unity with the divine, and actively choosing the thoughts and vibrations that shape your reality. This chapter emphasizes the power of choice and responsibility in shaping a life of freedom, joy, and creation.

5. Personal and Spiritual Growth

"Contrary to this, the essence of the mind mirroring technique is not to catalyze a change or to become different. It is, in fact, an invitation to embrace continuity and sameness, which paradoxically can lead to the most profound transformations. It's about shedding the layers of pretense and the exhausting endeavor of trying to be something we're not."

Growth, particularly in the context of personal or psychological development, involves an ongoing process of self-improvement, self-discovery, and the expansion of one's capabilities and understanding. Every human being comes into the world with a unique set of potentials. This includes innate abilities, talents, predispositions, and capacities. Human growth involves the actualization of these inherent qualities. This concept encompasses several key elements:

Consider the acorn, the quintessence of potentiality. Recognizable for its inherent capability, once planted, it unfurls into the grandeur of an oak. The tree's growth, maturity, and eventual decline are the manifestations of its potential. Living entities alone possess potential, contingent upon self-direction, the faculty of choice, and control over one's existence. Human beings, as living systems, cannot simply be altered—they must grow, thereby actualizing their individual essence. Each person is imbued with potential, though it can be stifled or diverted.

Self-actualization is the pursuit of reaching one's full potential and becoming the most that one can be. This concept, famously highlighted by Abraham Maslow, is placed at the apex of his hierarchy of needs and represents the culmination of fulfilling one's innate potential. Growth in this sense fosters a mindset that is open to new experiences and challenges, continuously seeking to expand one's horizons.

Emotional maturity is integral to growth, encompassing the development of greater awareness and management of one's emotions, resilience, and the capacity for empathy and compassion. Emotional growth involves becoming more attuned to both one's own emotions and those of others.

Self-transformation as part of growth involves a shift in identity from the limitations of one's self-image to an expanded sense of possibilities. Transformative changes serve to align one's actions with one's inner values and aspirations. This could manifest in changing habits, re-evaluating beliefs, or making life changes that reflect one's true self.

In essence, to grow means to engage in a lifelong journey of development, striving to activate and make the most out of one's innate potential. It is not a destination but a continuous path of becoming more expansive, wise, skilled, and compassionate.

The Journey of Growth

From the moment of your conception to the inevitability of death, your life is a journey of growth. The body's physical development from infancy to adulthood is evident, showcasing a continuous evolution of form and ability. But your growth is also signified by cycles of evolution into higher states of consciousness. A higher state of consciousness is represented by expanded awareness, wholeness, and fulfillment of potential.

Every cycle of action and experience that you engage and complete is a fundamental unit for unlocking your potential. These cycles of experience build upon each other, reaching ever-greater depths and heights of understanding, much like ascending a spiral staircase of enlightenment.

The pace at which we process our experiences is reflective of our growth trajectory. The quicker we assimilate life's lessons, the faster we evolve.

Yet, growth cannot be hastened beyond its natural rhythm. It is by relinquishing resistance, by allowing experiences to run their natural course, that they reach fruition. Every aspect of our lives, each encounter, and every action has its own tempo to completion. Yet it is in completion that we grow an increment. Should our experiences remain incomplete, life, in its wisdom, tends to present recurring themes, offering us chances to fully engage with and resolve them. With each cycle of completion, we're transformed, and primed to face future challenges with greater confidence and depth.

Understanding life's dynamism is freeing. Observing how life's patterns align with our personal growth, skill development, and joy is to see the intricate dance of existence. Though potential exists beyond time's confines, it can only manifest in the temporal dance with life, in the immediacy of the present.

This personal evolution towards wholeness and fulfillment is a reflection of the divine within us, instilling humility as we tap into the infinite potential of our growth. Contemplation on this notion reshapes our sense of self.

Awareness of the boundless nature of our potential aligns with our sense of divinity without creating a chasm between the creator and creation. Even though the full extent of our potential is beyond comprehension, the existence of our potential is revealed as we live our everyday lives as we intuitively move toward completion. We celebrate the unfolding, the blooming of life within us, and the actualization of potential, whether its baking a cake, excelling in a chosen field, dancing, or simply smiling.

Potential is timeless, yet its realization is a moment of triumph, as tangible as the intricate design of a leaf or the joy in a child's laughter. While our conceptual capacities may have limits, our capacity for observation and awareness does not. Striving to extend our current level of awareness taps into an infinite source within us, promising totality.

Awareness is within your grasp; otherwise, the concept would not exist. Potential inherently propels forward, and stagnation is but a temporary illusion. Limiting our potential merely diverts the energy needed for its continuous activation. Life is a response to the perpetual flux of circumstances, and meeting these changes requires a shift in our awareness and abilities, fueling the creative fire of existence. Happiness, then, is the natural state of a being engaged in ceaseless creation and completion.

It all begins with observation. Our response to life's tapestry is woven from three threads: direct contact with the present situation, a clear perception of the unfolding event, and a keen understanding of its significance in fulfilling our growth potential.

Growth encompasses both potential and the process it entails. Without potential, there is no process; and potential, by its nature, is independent. Our role is to activate this potential, recognizing that every life event is a step in this activation, and in the dynamic of wholeness, we see the culmination of a process where energy brings potential to life.

As you navigate the journey of growth, envision it not as a circular path leading back to where you began, but as an ascending spiral. Each loop of the spiral represents the completion of an action or pattern propelling you to a higher level of consciousness and expanded awareness. This spiral progression suggests that with every turn, you are advancing, developing further complexity and nuance in your understanding and capabilities.

The completion of every cycle of action and experience within this spiral is a step upward. Whether the increments of ascent are minuscule or significant, the trajectory remains upward. This vertical climb signifies permanent advancement, a contrast to the cyclical patterns of daily experiences that are more ephemeral. At the apex of this spiral, you find the fullest activation of your potential—where possibility becomes a tangible reality, driving the entire progression.

Life, in its vast omniscience, equips us with what we need for growth at any given moment. The circumstances we encounter inherently possess the wisdom of life's grand design. Even when situations seem harsh or adverse, they may be necessary corrections for previous imbalances or increased challenges due to previous avoidance. Life's omniscience is embedded within every situation, containing the very lessons and tools required for furthering the activation of our potential.

In this light, growth is not a mere accumulation of experiences but a continuous upward evolution toward higher states of being and understanding. It is an engagement with life's inherent wisdom, confronting and embracing challenges that refine and define our essence.

6. The Spirituality of Mind Mirroring

"Yet, as I assume the role of the mirror, I find myself stepping out from under the shadow of these thoughts, emerging into the clear light of being. The mirroring process allows me to observe these attacks not as truths but as the ego's noise, separate from the core of my identity. In this space, the ego's voice loses its power, disarmed by the simple act of recognition and non-engagement. I am no longer entangled in its web of criticism; I am simply present, observing, and existing without the need for defense or justification. This is the sanctuary of the mirror—a tranquil realm where being is enough."

The essence of the Mind Mirroring technique is rooted in spiritual purity, where your mind becomes a clear mirror, reflecting wholeness and the holiness of your Creator. In this reflection, there is no distortion, only the luminous truth of who you are manifesting in the world through your thoughts and actions. As you become the mirror of your mind, the divine shines through without obstruction, extending healing and wholeness.

In this state, holiness is not just mirrored but becomes the very nature of our existence, merging the reflection with reality. You, as a mirror of truth, hold the light of God within, shining brilliantly, undimmed by ego or illusion. By allowing the divine to illuminate through you, you transcend the bounds of time and touch eternity.

The holy mind reflects love and loveliness, transforming perceptions of pain into peace and mortality into everlasting life. By aligning with the divine, errors and grievances dissolve, revealing the sanctity in ourselves and others. Committing to this reflection, even if just for a focused ten minutes, can transfigure your understanding and deepen your connection with the love and joy of God's presence.

This technique teaches us that our fellow human beings are mirrors of our own self-image; as we perceive them, so we perceive ourselves. Let awareness not reflect a fragmented mind, but instead, let the whole mind interpret and reveal the health and wholeness inherent in all. In identifying with the mirror within, we recognize the completeness that we are a part of, which is the love of God.

The world is a mirror of your inner state; release it from illusions, and you liberate yourself. Perception reflects mindset, not reality. By choosing to see the world through the mirror of the divine, you offer it, and yourself, a miraculous vision of God's eternal love. This process in the mind is the key to salvation: what is seen outside mirrors the inner sanctum of the mind, heralding the forgiveness and grace of the divine.

In a state where nothing obstructs the direct connection between God and His creations, or between His children and their true selves, the understanding of creation remains unending. The images and ideas you welcome into your mind's mirror might either draw you closer to or further from the concept of eternity. Yet, eternity itself exists outside the bounds of time. By reaching beyond the temporal realm, and embracing its reflection within you, you move from the temporal to the sacred. Just as surely as a reflection of sanctity inspires all to relinquish guilt, embracing this reflection will guide you toward a divine state of being. Manifest the tranquility of the divine in this world, thereby elevating it to a heavenly plane. The reflection of actuality attracts all to the truth, and in embracing it, they move beyond mere reflections.

The concept of God or a higher power is deeply personal and varies significantly across cultures, religions, and individual beliefs. In many traditions, God is seen as the ultimate reality or truth, the source of all love, and the ultimate healer or guide towards growth and fulfillment. Here's how God and its attributes might relate to various aspects of the human experience and therapeutic processes:

Love

In your spiritual journey, you might find that love is often seen as a reflection of the divine, going beyond simple emotions to forge a deep, universal bond. This divine love shows up in your life in many ways – the warmth you feel in romantic relationships, the care in family bonds, the support among friends, and most powerfully, in the form of unconditional love. It's a crucial part of your experience as a human, showcasing your ability to forge deep and meaningful connections.

Think of love as more than just a feeling. It's a vital part of your existence, weaving through every aspect of your life. It's how you engage with the world around you – accepting, being fully present, and respecting everything and everyone in it. Imagine being in a situation where, instead of dwelling on past mistakes or worrying about the future, you choose to fully immerse yourself in the present, appreciating every aspect of your current experience.

Consider how love's essence extends beyond your personal emotions. When you feel empathy and compassion for others, even strangers, you're tapping into this universal love. It's like those moments when you help someone without expecting anything in return or when you deeply understand someone else's struggles. This kind of love acknowledges the interconnectedness of all life, promoting growth and nurturing potential, not just within yourself but in your community as well. It transcends personal gains, fostering a sense of unity and shared humanity. A crucial aspect of this love is forgiveness, where you learn to accept imperfections, in yourself and others, and let go of past hurts. Through this, we cultivate a deeper sense of patience and tolerance. Unconditional love, the most profound expression of this divine essence, remains steady and unwavering regardless of the situation, epitomizing love in its purest form, and it nurtures a lasting bond that transcends time and space.

Peace

You might discover that inner peace often stems from a deep connection with something greater than yourself – be it a higher power or a profound sense of purpose. This kind of peace isn't just the absence of external noise or conflict; it's a steady state of calm and tranquility within you, regardless of what's happening around you. It's about finding satisfaction and gratitude in your life as it is right now, appreciating the present without yearning for more or different.

For example, imagine you're in a stressful work situation. Instead of getting swept up in anxiety or frustration, you manage to stay calm and composed. This balance isn't just helpful in that moment; it also helps you bounce back more quickly from setbacks, maintaining a positive outlook even when things get tough.

Achieving this peace means accepting things as they are – including accepting yourself and others without resistance. It's about being present in the moment, observing your thoughts and feelings without judgment. This is where practices like meditation or Mind Mirroring come in. They aren't just passive exercises; they're active steps towards cultivating a state of internal harmony that positively impacts all aspects of your life, emotionally, psychologically, and spiritually.

In everyday life, this could look like choosing to focus on the positive in a challenging situation, or taking a moment to breathe and center yourself before responding to a difficult matter. It's about creating a foundation of stability and contentment within yourself, no matter what's happening outside.

Joy

You might find that joy is more than just fleeting happiness; it's a deep-seated state that makes life richer and more fulfilling. You can cultivate this joy through close relationships, engaging in activities you love, practicing gratitude, and maintaining a positive attitude. It's like feeling an inner glow of energy and enthusiasm, a sense of contentment that lasts longer than momentary pleasures.

For instance, consider the joy you feel when spending time with loved ones, engaging in a hobby you're passionate about, or simply reflecting on the things you're grateful for in your life. This joy is often visible in your actions and expressions, like when you can't help but smile or laugh while sharing a joke with a friend. It brings a sense of liveliness and engagement with the world around you.

Joy also fosters an optimistic view of life. It encourages you to see the bright side of things and maintain hope for the future. This state of mind leads you to embrace spontaneity and playfulness, to find pleasure in the simple things. It's about feeling alive and connected, whether you're enjoying a beautiful sunset or celebrating a personal achievement.

Many see joy as a divine gift, a celebration of life's blessings. It comes from both external events and internal realizations, nurtured by an appreciation of life's moments and a heartfelt sense of gratitude. In everyday life, joy can be as simple as the warmth you feel when helping a stranger or the satisfaction of completing a project. It's a vital part of what makes life truly enriching and worthwhile.

Light

Spiritual light in your life might represent a deep, transformative journey that goes beyond the ordinary. It's like an inner beacon guiding you towards greater wisdom, self-awareness, and connection with something larger than yourself. This could be a connection to the divine, the universe, or a broader spiritual reality.

For example, you might experience moments of clarity and

understanding that feel like a light has been turned on in your mind, illuminating paths and choices that were previously unclear. These moments can feel like a new beginning, much like how the dawn signals the start of a new day.

This spiritual light can also be about discovering and awakening your true self or soul. It could manifest in those profound moments of self-realization during meditation, or when you're deeply moved by a piece of music or art, feeling a connection to something much larger than yourself. It's like those times when you feel an overwhelming sense of unity with the world around you, an understanding that you're part of a vast, interconnected universe.

In everyday life, you might find this spiritual light in moments of deep reflection or when you're overcome by a sense of peace and oneness during a walk in nature or in quiet contemplation. These experiences can feel like glimpses into a deeper, more mystical aspect of existence, where you feel a profound connection to all life and the universe as a whole.

Creativity

Creativity in your life might be much more than a skill or talent; it can be your personal connection to something divine or transcendent. Imagine that within you, there's a spark of divine essence. When you engage in creative activities, whether it's painting, writing, gardening, or even cooking, you're bringing out this inner divinity. It's like you're contributing to the universe's ongoing creation, aligning with that same force that sparked life.

Think of the universe as a masterpiece of divine intelligence, and your own creativity as a reflection of this grand creator's work. Have you ever been so immersed in a creative task that you felt guided by something beyond your usual thinking? That's like channeling wisdom, beauty, or truth from a higher plane.

Your creativity can bridge gaps between cultures and languages, connecting you to others and the divine in a deep, unspoken way. It's about uncovering unity and harmony that underlie our apparent differences.

For instance, when you create something, you might experience moments of profound insight, feeling like you've tapped into a deeper reality. This process can be incredibly fulfilling, bringing you a sense of joy and bliss that feels almost divine. It's like tapping into an endless wellspring of potential, reflecting the boundless nature of whatever you perceive as divine. In this way, your creative acts become sacred, aligning your personal expression with the universal process of creation and existence.

Connection

In your life, the idea of "oneness" might resonate as a feeling of deep connection with everything around you. This belief, central to many spiritual paths, suggests that beneath the surface, all things in the universe are interconnected and depend on each other. This isn't just about physical things; it extends to your emotions, your spirit, and even the metaphysical aspects of life. Each element you encounter, from the people you meet to the natural world around you, is a part of this divine tapestry.

Imagine you're walking in a forest. As you observe the trees, animals, and the sky above, you sense that everything, including you, is part of a larger whole. This sensation challenges the usual feeling of being separate from your surroundings. Many spiritual teachings suggest that the boundaries we perceive between ourselves and others, or between the material and spiritual, are illusions. Recognizing this oneness can lead to a profound understanding of interconnectedness, where showing kindness to others is also a way of loving yourself.

You might have moments in life, perhaps while meditating or in nature, where you feel a strong unity with everything, filled with peace, joy, and an expanded awareness. Achieving this often means moving beyond your ego, the part of you that feels separate and distinct, and embracing a sense of unity with all existence.

This realization brings a deep respect for all life, seeing every part of the world as sacred. You start to view the people, animals, and even the trees and rivers around you as divine expressions. Such experiences can bring a profound inner peace, a contentment that comes from letting go of personal wants, fears, and conflicts.

Ultimately, oneness with the divine is about transcending perceived separations, revealing a harmonious connection with the essence that flows through the entire universe. It's a state of consciousness where you feel a deep bond not just with the people close to you, but with all of existence.

Transformation

In your everyday life, spiritual transformation can be like embarking on a profound journey of personal change, deeply connected to a sense of something greater than yourself, perhaps the divine or a higher power. This journey often starts with a moment of awakening, where suddenly, things make sense in a new way. It could be during a quiet moment of reflection, a walk in nature, or even during a challenging time, when you suddenly realize there's more to life and yourself than you previously thought. This new awareness often leads to a broader perspective, where you start to feel more empathy for others and a stronger connection to the world around you, seeing the sacredness in everyday life.

You might have moments that feel like direct encounters with something divine. These could be deeply moving experiences, profound realizations, or moments of intense love and connection that make you feel reborn, giving you a fresh outlook and deeper understanding of yourself.

A big part of this transformation is finding inner peace and harmony, a sense of being in sync with life's flow, not just avoiding conflict. It's about how you live each day, bringing those spiritual insights into your daily routine. This could mean making more mindful choices, living in a way that aligns with your spiritual values, or finding something sacred and meaningful in ordinary activities like gardening, cooking, or spending time with loved ones.

Remember, this isn't just a one-off experience but a continuous journey, growing and deepening your connection with the divine or your spiritual understanding. For those who believe, this divine presence becomes a part of everything in life, offering guidance, comfort, and a sense of purpose. In a therapeutic context, embracing this spiritual dimension can be key to holistic care, helping you navigate life's challenges and promoting healing and personal growth. This transformative journey highlights the significant role spirituality plays in enriching and deepening our human experience.

The Transformative Results of Mind Mirroring

As you practice Mind Mirroring, you'll notice a ripple effect. Your listening skills will sharpen, not just for your internal dialogues but in your interactions with others. Authenticity in self-expression becomes the norm, and you discover a more genuine version of yourself. You are free to be you. You will navigate through your internal struggles more effectively, and in doing so, you will clear the fog that often clouds the mind.

Through Mind Mirroring, you align more closely with your essence — a divine being experiencing human existence. You come to know yourself not as an amalgamation of thoughts and experiences, but as presence, as being itself. And in that knowing, you find the clarity and peace that come from within, a true testament to the inner therapist you have embraced.

Maybe today, or perhaps tomorrow, you will witness a profound change within yourself through this process, like seeing a transformed reflection in a mirror. When the time is right, you'll discover this new version of you, nestled in the depths of your mind, ready to be acknowledged. Gazing into this metaphorical mirror, you'll come to realize that the radiance and beauty you see are indeed aspects of yourself. Consider this practice a tribute to the divine, confident in the knowledge that it will be reciprocated with a form of love beyond your current comprehension, a joy too profound to fully grasp, and a vision too sacred for mere physical sight. Yet, be assured that at some point — perhaps even today or tomorrow — you will come to a deeper understanding, appreciation, and vision of these truths.

7. The Nuts and Bolts of Mind Mirroring

"Through this practice, I am learning to recognize and observe these thoughts—thoughts that would otherwise go unacknowledged, as they quietly influence my perception and experience of life. By embodying these internal characters, I begin to watch them fade, not actively trying to change them, but through the passive act of awareness. This is the gift of the exercise: not in seeking transformation, but in the natural unfolding of a more present and open-hearted existence."

The Mind Mirroring technique is simple and requires no special learning beyond the setup of the session and the actual engagement in the process. The length of time that you engage is organically determined, however, a minimum of 10 minutes gives you enough time to "get into it." As you participate in the process, you will come to appreciate the time that you spend with yourself, like the time that you spend with a dear friend. The only action that you'll be engaged with is the process of speaking and listening. Remember, this process is not so much about the content of what you say as it is about the reflection of whatever you speak.

Setting up a Mind Mirroring Session

1. Choosing the Space: Identify a private area where you can be undisturbed and where your voice won't carry to unintended ears. This space is your stage, sacred for introspection, and must be respected as such.

2. Arranging the Chairs: Position two matching straight-back, armless chairs facing each other. This can be done with the chairs almost touching at the corners, forming a slight diagonal. This arrangement facilitates ease of movement between the 'speaker' chair (where you start) and the 'mirror' chair (which serves as your reflective counterpart). You will be switching chairs fairly rapidly and frequently.

3. Initiating the Session: Begin seated, facing the empty mirror chair. Start with *one word or sentence* that simply names your inner state. This one word or sentence is the beginning of your mind-mirroring conversation. The sentence can be a statement, a question, a command, or an exclamation!

4. Mirroring the Dialogue: Immediately after expressing this word or sentence, move to the mirror chair and echo your words back to the speaker chair precisely the way the speaker spoke them, capturing the spoken words, with the same body gestures and emotion. Do not add or subtract any words and no suggestions or advice.

5. Continuing the Conversation: Immediately after the mirrored response, switch back to the speaker chair and then speak whatever comes up for you in response to the mirrored words but *speak only one sentence.* As mirror, you are simply recreating the embodiment of your spoken words, and then as speaker, you are responding to these same words reflected by the mirror.

Limiting yourself to one line makes it easier to reflect (more on this below). Continue alternating between chairs, delivering and reflecting *one line at a time* and no more. While in the speaker chair, be patient without censoring whatever emerges in the moment. It will be anything.

A rhythm will naturally develop, signaling when to switch chairs but seek to switch chairs the moment you complete your sentence, keeping it going, back and forth for about ten minutes minimum. There may be some pauses and that's okay. Whatever words come out are always the perfect words. You don't even need to make sense and you may jump from one thing to another. Trust the flow but keep it at one sentence. There's no need to rush. The conversation will have its own organic endpoint. You will stop when you choose to stop, and you might go much longer than ten minutes.

6. Concluding with Gratitude: When you sense the dialogue is complete, speak gratitude towards the empty chair for its role in your reflective journey, *"Thank you for reflecting me."*

Remember, this is not a performance for an external audience but a private session for self-discovery and affirmation. Through this process, you will sharpen your ability to listen deeply—not just to the words spoken but to the unspoken language of your being. Each Mind Mirroring session is an improvisation of the self, a unique and spontaneous journey into the heart of your internal dialogue. There is no rehearsing or pretense. Mind Mirroring is truly a "come as you are" party.

The Cast of Internal Characters

The mind is indeed a stage, and the cast of characters within it are multifaceted and transient aspects of our inner selves, each playing a role in the personal narratives we create and live by. This psychological troupe consists of internal voices, each with a distinctive part to play in our mental theatre, often reflecting the complexities of our emotional landscape shifting and changing in a moment.

While it is not necessary to name, describe, or predefine these inner voices (but rather *embody* these voices as they emerge in the moment), the range of descriptors of the many voices is many and varied. On the negative side is the judge, the critic, or the bully. On the positive side is the worthy, the confident, or 'I'm okay' voices. These voices could be questioning voices, or exclamations or commands. The voices you speak and how you speak them are yours to play and you get to play them however they show up in the moment.

These characters are not merely disruptors; they are an integral part of our internal dialogue. They embody our doubts, fears, guilts, and vulnerabilities. Yet, in the grand narrative of our inner world, these characters can also offer a chance for dialogue and understanding. By listening to and embodying them, we can learn about our insecurities and desires, our reflexive responses to pain, and our deepest yearnings for acceptance and love.

In therapy, especially within the realm of Mind Mirroring, one learns to engage with these characters, to hear them out, to acknowledge and challenge them, and to integrate their perspectives into a more compassionate and cohesive self-understanding. This process is not about silencing the drama but about becoming a skilled director who can harmonize the ensemble of internal voices into a narrative that supports personal growth and emotional well-being.

Mind Mirroring Modes of Listening

In Mind Mirroring sessions, the approach to speaking is spontaneous and unrehearsed. As the speaker, you simply take a seat and express whatever comes into awareness, focusing on speaking one sentence at a time. This method doesn't require any 'correctness' of expression or a pre-set conversation topic. The essence of these sessions lies in your freedom to be and to speak openly, without concern for external judgment. Your primary objective is to accurately reflect your own words and emotions. This pure reflection is the key function of the mirror during the session. There are, however, a couple of variations in the mode of listening that still honor the pure reflective function of the mirror.

Mind Mirroring involves adopting the role of both the speaker and the listener. As the listener, or the 'mirror', your task is to reflect the words precisely as spoken, without altering or interpreting them. Here are the specific modes of listening used in Mind Mirroring:

1. **Exact Echoing:** This is the primary listening mode in Mind Mirroring. Here, you replicate the speaker's words and

emotions precisely as they were expressed. For instance, if the speaker says, *"I don't know what to say,"* you mirror this statement verbatim, with the same tone and gestures.

2. **'I' and 'You' Shifting:** In this mode, the mirror might shift the pronouns when reflecting the speaker's words. If the speaker says, *"I don't know what to say,"* as the mirror you might respond with, *"You don't know what to say,"* maintaining the original emotional tone and gestures. This mode highlights the interchangeable nature of 'I' and 'You', leading to a realization of unity between the speaker and the mirror.

3. **Using the Phrase *"I'm Hearing You Say..."*:** In this approach, the mirror acknowledges what the speaker has said by prefacing their reflection with, *"I'm hearing you say..."* For example, if the speaker says, *"I don't know what to say,"* the mirror responds with, *"I'm hearing you say, 'I don't know what to say,'"* or *"I'm hearing you say, 'You don't know what to say,'"* This phrase serves as an intellectual acknowledgment that the speaker has been heard and understood.

4. **Silence:** At times during a Mind Mirroring session, you may simply want to speak out loud such as in a stream of consciousness without any immediate reflection. It's okay to babble on about nothing. As you do this you might become aware of certain insights and realizations. When you feel the timing is right, you can switch over to the mirror chair and reflect only the last few words.

These listening modes in Mind Mirroring not only facilitate a deeper self-reflection but also enhance your understanding of the unity between yourself and others. As you become proficient in this technique, you can creatively alternate between these listening modes within a single session, enriching the experience and discovering the interconnectedness in your daily interactions with others.

8. Improvising the Mind: Embracing Spontaneity

"There are moments where this introspection makes me question my self-identity, for the experience it provides is nothing short of extraordinary. It's like stepping into a state of 'no mind,' where presence is pure and unadulterated, where the concept of 'I' as a body dissolves into the ether. In this space, existence is no longer tied to the physical form but is an expansive beingness."

Improv is created on-the-spot theater. It often begins with a word, a phrase, or a premise and then flowers into a full-blown scene or play. Improv is *play* in the true sense of the word. Play is spontaneous, unrehearsed action and dialogue. Play exists between people. Watch children together and you will see how they naturally play without reservation or forethought. Actors in an improv scene play *off* each other and play *with* each other. It is give-and-take, a true exchange of energy. In improv, the actors are creators on the go. They are creating the scene and the dialogue as they go along, and they never really know where things will go. There is no final product except the ending of a scene. And then it's over.

The improv process is the same as the life process. Shakespeare said it well. The whole world is a stage where men and women play their parts. We enter the scene of our lives at birth and then we exit at death, and everything in between is where we play our part. Life is a series of scenes and encounters within the various environments of our lives which includes family, friends, and work relationships. We are *creating* our lives as we go along, and we *bring into* our lives certain relationships and scenes. And that is where the human drama gets acted out.

Within the various contexts of our lives, there is also another drama going on. It occurs on the private stage of the mind. We talk to ourselves sub vocally and sometimes out loud. In fact, what we take as "thinking" is nothing more than spontaneous dialogue that occurs between parts of ourselves. And the speakers in these conversations have their character qualities such as the judge, the critic, the whiner, the domineering, the victim, or the helpless to name a few. The dramas we experience in our external world truly represent the drama that is going on in our internal world. Are we listening to our minds?

Listening is at the heart of the improv principle, *"yes, and...."*

This brings us full circle to what Mind Mirroring is all about. Mind Mirroring is a technique where you get to play out the inner drama of your mind. You get to speak and listen to yourself. As in any improv scene, you create the dialogue, and through mirroring you become the inner audience who is simply listening to what is being spoken. And it all starts with a single word or phrase.

Mind mirroring is not meant to be performed in front of an audience although that could be an interesting scenario to see how that might unfold. The purpose of mind mirroring is to *know* yourself, to *speak* yourself, to *be* yourself. With mind mirroring, you are not performing. You are not acting. You are *being*. You are being *you* and you are being *yourself.* You become your own audience. You get to watch and listen to the mind and come to realize you are the creator of your thinking.

Where does Mind Mirroring start? As an open improv scene starts from nothing, so does a Mind Mirroring scene start from nothing. It starts the moment you sit in front of the empty chair. It matters little what is spoken or in what "character" or with what emotion. It is not about the content of what is said. It is about mirroring what was just spoken, and *how* it was spoken, in the here and now.

In the realm of human experience, the art of Mind Mirroring aligns closely with the principles of improvisational theater, encapsulating the spontaneous and unscripted nature of our everyday situations along with our mental and emotional landscapes. This chapter delves into how Mind Mirroring facilitates a deeper understanding of the self, mirroring the unpredictable, improvisational essence of life. In fact, a Mind Mirroring session replicates the exact nature of an improvisational scene except the audience, characters, and dialogue are all rolled into one.

The Nature of Internal Dialogue

Our minds are a stage for an ongoing, unscripted dialogue. This internal conversation is an interplay of various psychological 'characters' such as the inner critic, the victim, the optimist, or the skeptic. These characters engage in a dynamic exchange, reflecting and shaping our perception of the external world. However, it begs the question – how often do we actively listen to this rich internal discourse?

In both improvisational theater and life, active listening is fundamental. It's not just about hearing words; it's about inviting and acknowledging what shows up in the moment, giving them space to unfold. In Mind Mirroring, this is achieved through a 'yes, and...' approach, that is, the mirror is accepting everything that is offered to it. This method involves speaking one's thoughts out loud and then actively listening, echoing the thoughts without judgment or modification, embodying a spirit of acceptance and continuation.

The practice of Mind Mirroring begins with an empty chair, symbolizing the stage for one's internal drama. In this space, a person articulates their thoughts, then shifts to the mirror position, echoing their own words. This process transcends performance; it's an exercise in presence and authenticity. The empty chair is not a critic but a representation of one's true self, a medium to confront and embrace one's unfiltered thoughts and feelings.

From Listening to Understanding

As improv work develops a person's listening ability so does Mind Mirroring, not through deliberate effort but by naturally being more present in conversations. The technique sharpens the distinction between speaking actively, which roots us in the present, and speaking *about* things, which often detracts from the immediacy of the moment. Active speaking and listening engender a genuine connection, both with oneself and with others.

Mind Mirroring, much like improv, teaches the value of spontaneity and presence. It encourages embracing the concept of 'being' amidst our human narratives. In our daily lives, just as on the improv stage, we encounter unforeseen scenarios, unexpected emotions, and unscripted moments. By applying the principles of Mind Mirroring, we learn to navigate life with greater ease, adaptability, and awareness.

Improv is all about being in the moment which intersects with the principles of Gestalt therapy, emphasizing awareness, the here and now, and the wholeness of experience. Improv is about creating in the moment, realizing that this moment is always occurring for the first time. Mind Mirroring, akin to Gestalt's focus on the present moment and personal responsibility, encourages a holistic understanding of one's thoughts and emotions, facilitating a more integrated and authentic self.

As one continues to practice Mind Mirroring, they experience a profound shift in their internal dialogue and ability to respond to situations more effectively and spontaneously as they occur. Every situation of daily living is an improv scene that is occurring for the very first time. Mind Mirroring, as well as improv, promotes a deeper self-awareness, a clearer understanding of one's mental patterns, and an enhanced capacity for spontaneity and empathy. It leads to a more mindful existence, where one is fully engaged in the richness of the present moment, both internally and externally.

In summary, Mind Mirroring is more than a therapeutic technique; it is a journey toward wholeness, presence, and authenticity. By embracing the improvisational nature of our minds, we open ourselves to a world of spontaneity, deeper understanding, and genuine connection. Through this practice, we not only become adept at navigating the internal landscapes of our psyche but also enhance our interactions with the world, making each moment a true reflection of our being.

9. The Human Encounter

"In practicing this technique, I've become acutely aware of the persistent voice of my ego—its barrage of self-judgments that launch relentless assaults on my being. This voice cloaks itself in various guises, echoing sentiments like "I'm not good enough," "I'm terrible," or "I shouldn't have said that," all converging into a singular, corrosive mantra: "I shouldn't exist." It's a stark realization that the ego's modus operandi is to attack existence itself, to undermine the very essence of being."

Human communication is a complex and nuanced dance, often taking the form of conversations, encounters, or dialogues. These interactions range from planned discussions to spontaneous exchanges, each representing unique moments of connection. In these encounters, individuals share their experiences, expectations, thoughts, and feelings on various topics, with each interaction being distinct and evolving based on the purpose, context, and relationship dynamics. Unfinished encounters often linger in one's mind, seeking resolution.

These exchanges, whether brief and surface-level or deep and extended, like those in therapy, are fundamental to our social structure. They go beyond mere word exchanges, weaving the intricate tapestry of human connection and understanding. Often, these interactions are complicated by unspoken expectations or demands one person may have of another.

This chapter explores the complex nature of human encounters, going beyond just the content of interactions. It sheds light on the various components that make up these exchanges. Additionally, this exploration lays the groundwork for understanding the introspective journey of the Mind Mirroring exercise, where you engage in deep self-dialogue. This chapter aims to connect the external world of interpersonal interactions with the inner world of self-discovery and understanding.

Context and Purpose of Conversation

Every conversation is an interactive cycle involving two or more people, encompassing a beginning, middle, and end. The common denominator in every interaction is the exchange of words that depict the various experiences of the individuals involved. The context significantly shapes its substance and direction. The nuances of a casual social conversation differ markedly from those of a formal business meeting, a family talk, or a therapeutic dialogue. Each conversation type is distinct, molded by the nature of the relationship and the situation, and driven by its own theme and purpose.

Participants in a conversation contribute pieces of themselves, evident in their choice of words and how they speak. Silence also plays a crucial role, serving as a powerful non-verbal element in the exchange. Conversations are arenas where a range of thoughts and feelings are expressed, showcasing various levels of awareness. The true skill in conversation lies in maintaining a balance between speaking and listening, a feat that is often challenged. Conversations can sometimes become dominated by one person trying to persuade another, or they may devolve into disorderly interactions with frequent interruptions. Such dynamics can hinder effective communication, highlighting the importance of mindful participation in conversations.

The Symbolic Nature of Words

Words are, at their core, symbols that represent experiences, beliefs, and perspectives, but they do not encapsulate the entirety of reality. Similar to how a map depicts a territory but is not the territory itself, words are mere representations of the actual entities or experiences they describe.

When we articulate our thoughts or recount past experiences, we are essentially reconstructing memories or interpretations of those events. The original events have passed, and although the present moment is experienced in real-time, it cannot be fully captured by language.

Words are tools for communication, but they should not be mistaken for the reality they attempt to portray. This distinction is important because there is a risk of becoming too absorbed in words, losing sight of the true nature of our experiences. Conversations, while focused on the present, often revolve around topics or ideas that are not present, such as past events or future plans. An encounter is a lived experience occurring in the present, distinct from the content of the conversation which often relates to the past or the future.

In daily life, conversations typically involve an exchange of information and viewpoints about various topics. Deeper, more introspective conversations, often found in therapeutic settings or moments of personal revelation, delve into the depths of personal experiences and emotions. In these dialogues, individuals attempt to articulate their inner experiences related to specific events, but the words used are not the experiences themselves. Each person uniquely experiences their own reality, and communication is the process of making others aware of these experiences. The reality of the present communication contrasts with the unreality of what is being communicated about.

Most conversations start with simple greetings or opening remarks and evolve depending on the participants and context. They frequently focus on past events or future expectations, seldom remaining anchored in the present moment, where life unfolds and reality is most acutely felt.

Human conversation is a complex and evolving landscape, shaped by the individual contexts, relationships, and personalities involved. Recognizing the symbolic nature of words and the intricacies of different modes of speaking enhances our ability to connect, understand, and effectively communicate our experiences with others.

Process of an Encounter

The art of conversation between two individuals is a multifaceted and evolving process, encompassing much more than the mere exchange of words. It involves a complex interplay of emotional, psychological, and social elements that are essential to human communication.

An encounter usually begins with a greeting, which sets the interaction's tone, whether it's a simple "hello," a handshake, a nod, or a culturally specific gesture. This initial phase might involve small talk or straightforward questions, serving as an icebreaker and setting the stage for the conversation's subject, which arises spontaneously.

Non-verbal cues like eye contact, body language, and facial expressions play a crucial role in these initial moments, helping to establish a connection and indicate openness to the conversation. As the encounter progresses into a back-and-forth exchange, participants take turns speaking and listening, sharing ideas, thoughts, and feelings in a balanced manner.

Effective listening goes beyond just hearing words; it requires active attention, understanding, and appropriate responses, which may include verbal acknowledgments or non-verbal cues such as nodding and observing the speaker's facial expressions. It's about being fully present and engaged with the speaker.

The conversation might stay focused on a specific topic or drift through various subjects, with each person contributing their perspective, knowledge, or emotions. Emotional undercurrents and psychological dynamics significantly influence the interaction, with empathy, understanding, and sensitivity to these non-verbal elements being crucial for meaningful communication.

As trust and comfort levels increase, participants may share more personal insights or stories, deepening the connection. Clarifying misunderstandings, providing feedback, or summarizing points are essential to ensure mutual understanding and respect.

Conversations can face challenges like misunderstandings or disagreements. The way these are addressed, whether through clarification, negotiation, or compromise, significantly impacts the outcome of the encounter.

Conversations ideally conclude naturally when the subjects have been thoroughly explored, and both parties feel heard and understood. This could be signaled by a pause in the conversation or mutual acknowledgment. The encounter often ends with a closing gesture, such as a summary, a thank-you, a handshake, or plans for future contact, providing a sense of closure.

Post-conversation, individuals typically reflect on the exchange, contemplating the content and their feelings, which can shape their understanding and influence future interactions.

In summary, a human encounter is a nuanced dance of speaking and listening, where emotional and psychological elements play a pivotal role. Effective communication within this process demands awareness, empathy, and respect, ensuring that both participants feel valued and understood.

Modes of Speaking in Human Interaction

In the complex realm of human communication, our modes of speaking play a crucial role in how we express and connect with others. Each mode serves a unique purpose, depending on context and situation, offering a window into our thoughts, feelings, and experiences, and thereby enhancing self-awareness and the quality of our interactions.

Speaking feelings, through phrases like *"I feel..."*, allows for the direct expression of emotions, adding authenticity and depth to our conversations. Speaking about an experience using *"I experience..."* shares personal reactions and perspectives, highlighting the subjective nature of our encounters with the world. When we say, *"I think..."* or *"I believe..."* we're sharing our opinions and beliefs, offering a glimpse into our cognitive processes.

Discussing physical sensations or discomforts, often encapsulated in speaking about the body, is key to conveying our physical state and well-being. Speaking awareness, through statements like *"I'm aware of..."* or *"I'm noticing..."*, demonstrates mindfulness and a conscious engagement with our surroundings and inner thoughts. Speaking insights, as in *"I realize..."*, often marks moments of personal discovery and understanding, reflecting growth and learning.

Narrating events or occurrences, or speaking about a situation, provides necessary context and background, setting the stage for a deeper understanding of the narrative. Speaking anticipations with phrases like *"I'm expecting..."* reveals our outlook on future events, while speaking about the future using *"I'm planning to..."* or *"I'm going to..."* indicates our intentions and goals.

Affirming our identity or state of being, as in speaking being with *"I am..."*, is fundamental to expressing who we are. Engaging in light conversation or chit-chat, known as 'speaking nothings', can serve as a social lubricant, easing us into more significant discussions. Speaking banter involves playful and light-hearted speech that often fosters a relaxed atmosphere.

Focused discussions on specific topics or subjects, or speaking 'about' something, are informative and often central to the exchange of ideas. Expressing dissatisfaction or discomfort, as in speaking complaining, *"This pisses me off"* can be negative but also important for sharing feelings. Similarly, speaking blaming, *("It's their fault")* by assigning responsibility to others can indicate a lack of personal accountability. Speaking words of judgment often begin with, *"They're so…"*.

Explaining or discussing ideas or theories, as in speaking concepts, is common in educational or intellectual contexts. Speaking ego, where the focus is excessively on oneself, can come across as self-centered. Expressing *"I want…", I desire…"* or *"I need…"* reveals our inner yearnings and aspirations.

Speaking preferences using *"I prefer…"* communicates our choices, while speaking intentions with *"I'm going to…"* signals decisive plans or actions. Making requests through *"Would you…"* showcases openness and a willingness to engage interdependently.

Speaking *'I'*, and including *'You'* in the speaking, addresses presence in the here-and-now. Saying the word, *'You'* brings presence into being. Saying the words *'I' and 'You'* brings us into intimate existence and the reality that we are one. Words like *"I love you"* and *"I appreciate you"* are rarely ever spoken except in the most intimate of our relationships.

Each mode of speaking opens a portal to communicate a certain aspect of self and has its unique place and function in our communications. By being aware of and skillful in utilizing these various modes, we can greatly enhance the effectiveness, richness, and depth of our interactions, fostering more nuanced and meaningful connections.

Modes of Listening

We often think of listening as a more passive process and somehow secondary to speaking. But without listening, there is no speaking. Without listening, speaking falls on deaf ears or turns into babbling. Listening isn't merely a receptacle for speaking; it invites and acknowledges speaking. It allows the speaker to come alive, exist, and flourish. Listening is an action that is way more active than it is passive.

Listening is acknowledging what is being heard.

Effective listening is a vital component of successful communication, and there are several modes through which an individual can convey to the speaker that they have been heard and understood. These modes encompass both verbal and nonverbal methods.

Effective listening is a multifaceted skill that involves various techniques to ensure that the speaker feels heard, understood, and validated. One key approach is reflecting back or paraphrasing, where you restate the speaker's words in your own language, often prefaced with phrases like *"So, what I am hearing is..."* or *"It sounds like you feel...".* This technique not only shows active listening but also aids in clarifying and confirming your understanding of the message.

Validating or acknowledging feelings is another critical aspect, where responses such as *"That sounds really challenging,"* or *"I can see why you'd feel that way,"* express empathy and recognition of the speaker's emotions and experiences. Asking clarifying questions like, *"Say some more about that."* or *"What happened next?"* is a straightforward yet effective way to show engagement and interest.

Nonverbal cues play a significant role too. Mirroring body language or emotions, through actions like nodding, maintaining eye contact, or reflecting the speaker's expressions, communicates attentiveness and empathy. Offering encouragement with phrases like *"Go on..."* or *"I'm listening..."* can be particularly effective when a speaker is hesitant or delving into difficult emotions. Making relational statements, such as *"I've felt that way before,"* or *"I can relate to that,"* fosters a sense of connection and understanding.

Expressing verbal affirmations with statements like *"I can understand that",* *"I see how that's important to you",* or *"That makes sense",* provides clear acknowledgment of the speaker's message. Nonverbal affirmations, including nodding or leaning forward, further signify engagement. Summarizing key points at the end of a conversation demonstrates that you have not only listened but also internalized and understood the shared information.

At times, silence can be a powerful tool, allowing the speaker space to express themselves fully without interruption. Facial expressions, such as concern, understanding, or interest, also convey emotional engagement. In certain relationships, physical gestures like a gentle touch or supportive pat can show empathy and understanding. In professional or academic settings, active note-taking shows that you are engaged and value the information being shared. Overall, these varied modes of listening enhance communication, fostering deeper understanding, connection, and empathy in conversations.

Incorporating these various modes of listening enhances communication, fostering deeper understanding, connection, and empathy in human encounters. Remember, effective listening is not just about the words you say in response; it's equally about your demeanor and approach to the conversation.

Mind Mirroring: A Dialogue with Self

In the practice of Mind Mirroring, this concept of encounter takes on an introspective dimension. Here, the encounter is not with another, but with oneself - the Self with a capital 'S', symbolizing the true essence of one's being. This true self represents the 'being' aspect of a 'human being', the core of your existence that is pure love and unconditional acceptance, the mirror itself. In Mind Mirroring, you engage in a conversation with this true Self as you *become* this true Self.

In this self-dialogue, the 'self' with a lowercase 's' – representing your human self with all its emotions, thoughts, and dramas – is mirrored back to you. This aspect of self, often intertwined with self-image and ego, is usually hidden from direct view because it is what we embody. However, through Mind Mirroring, you come to see this 'self' reflected back. The practice involves a genuine dialogue with yourself, where the mirror chair serves as a reflective surface, echoing only what has been spoken.

As you engage in Mind Mirroring, you exchange words with yourself, delving into a deep conversation with your mirror self. This process allows for a true dialogue, where your words, thoughts, and feelings are reflected back to you, facilitating self-awareness and discovery. Unlike typical conversations where each participant may go their separate ways, Mind Mirroring brings you closer to your inner self.

Mind Mirroring is thus characterized as an interactive journey of speaking and self-reflection. This practice enables a profound exploration of the self, where you not only converse but also listen and understand the depths of your being. Through Mind Mirroring, you embark on a transformative journey to know yourself as the mirror - the truest reflection of your whole self, unified as one with being itself.

10. Living Your Life as Mirror

"And yet, in this very lack of purpose, I discern a subtle yet profound shift. As I reflect on what I notice post-exercise, a clarity emerges: I find myself inhabiting the present more authentically. Through the act of mirroring my thoughts without the pressure to change them, I am inadvertently learning the art of presence. The technique guides me to a state of being that is deeply rooted in the here and now, fostering a newfound appreciation for the subtleties of the present moment."

As you practice Mind Mirroring, you are coming to know yourself as mirror embodying all the qualities and functions of a mirror. Living your life *as* mirror is a profound concept that can have significant implications for how you perceive and interact with the world. It's about embodying qualities of reflection, receptivity, and clarity in your daily existence without effort. Here's a deeper exploration of this idea:

Just as a mirror reflects whatever stands before it without judgment or alteration, living as mirror involves observing and experiencing life without immediately reacting, judging, or trying to change what you encounter. It's about being present and open to experiences as they unfold.

In this state, you approach life with a sense of openness and acceptance. You receive experiences, people, and thoughts as they are, rather than as you wish them to be. This doesn't mean you don't discern or express yourself, but rather that your first response is understanding and acceptance rather than resistance in how you think things should be.

Living as mirror also involves turning that reflective quality inward, cultivating self-awareness. By mirroring your own thoughts and feelings, you gain deeper insights into your own nature and motivations. You learn to truly listen to yourself.

Mirroring in relationships means deeply listening to and understanding others, reflecting back their emotions and thoughts in a way that makes them feel seen and heard. This can foster deeper connections and empathy.

A mirror doesn't distort; it shows things as they are. Similarly, living your life as mirror involves expressing clarity and truth, both in how you view the world and in your interactions with others.

This concept aligns closely with mindfulness, as it encourages living in the moment and fully engaging with the present situation as it unfolds, rather than getting lost in thoughts about the past or future.

Mirrors don't discriminate; they reflect all things equally. Applying this to life means striving for impartiality and equanimity in dealing with various situations and people.

Just as a mirror passively transforms its environment by the mere act of reflection, living as mirror suggests that you can effect change through the power of observation and presence, rather than through forceful action.

Mirrors balance light and reflection, creating harmony in their reflections. In life, this translates to seeking balance in your actions, thoughts, and emotions, aiming for a harmonious existence.

Finally, living as mirror involves embodying consistency and integrity in your actions and being true to yourself, reflecting your inner being as you engage with the external world. You step outside of the ego.

Living your life as mirror is a pathway to deeper understanding, compassion, and connection. It encourages a way of being that is centered on presence, awareness, and the authentic reflection of one's inner truth rather than an ego-centric way of living. You become who you are and discover there is no effort in being anything but what you are.

11. Tips, Tricks, and Perspectives

"There are so many "techniques" out there and methods for self-improvement, trying to change myself. I am coming to realize that change is already always happening and all I need do is go with the flow of my existence."

While following the structure of a Mind Mirroring session, there is much room for creativity, but the most important element to maintain throughout is the concept of the mirror and to become the reflection in the mirror. Listed below are a few ways to work with the flow and variations of a Mind Mirroring session.

1. It is good to start each session with just a word or sentence maintaining the one-sentence rule throughout. The one word or sentence simply names what is dominant in your consciousness. From there, a conversation or encounter ensues.

2. But with that said, at times, you might want to permit yourself to ramble on about something like a stream of consciousness, knowing that the mirror chair is listening. When you ramble on, you probably won't be able to replicate a whole stream of sentences, but you can replicate the last few words of the last sentence. That will be all there is to mirror.

3. You will always have something to say. Give yourself the space to speak whatever you speak. Mind mirroring is not about the content but rather the speaking and the listening.

4. You can do this process in front of a physical mirror, and it is just as powerful as with the two chairs. When you speak into a physical mirror, and then shift your psychological position, you are psychologically trading places, repeating what was just spoken. You experience the mirror talking back to you and

showing you how you are.

5. You can also do this process with your phone camera just as you would be looking into a mirror. You can always record the session and see what you learn from watching the recording.

6. You can get to the point where you can do this process "on the fly" without needing to set up a two-chair situation. When you are alone and hear a thought, simply repeat that thought aloud, the way you are hearing it in your mind.

7. You can also do it silently just as you are silently speaking these words as you are reading them.

8. You can do this anywhere, anytime except in company. It goes without saying that if you do it with others who would have no idea what you are doing you might well be considered crazy.

9. One of the main barriers to get over is the seeming ridiculousness of this technique which is teaching you to talk to yourself out loud. But that is the whole idea—to vocalize the thoughts that you are already speaking on the private stage of your mind, which is no less ridiculous.

10. This work is also a commitment, a commitment to yourself, just as you would commit to a therapy situation. You are committing to your own growth and potential. How frequently you do it is up to you.

11. You will experience insights and realizations as you go along, some of which you can put into words and some which you can't. One insight that is guaranteed is the awareness that you are *being* itself, that being is your true identity. You are not a 'human being'; you are a 'being human'.

12. You will notice some shifts in your own behavior and spontaneity when you are with others.

13. You'll notice resistance to doing the exercise. These are the same resistances we all have in honestly facing ourselves.

14. Sometimes it is good to make an appointment with yourself

anytime between now and later. Or when the moment is appropriate, just check in with yourself to say, 'hello' is all that's needed.

15. Sometimes you might just make a gesture without words (e.g. stroking your chin, taking a deep breath, or shaking your head); mirror that gesture just the way you did it.

16. This technique is not about trying to change anything or become 'better' but rather allowing changes to occur of their own accord. And they will, and not the way you think.

17. You will always be how you are, except you will be shedding the thought processes that keep you hidden and limited.

18. Thoughts are nothing but words that you tell yourself and pictures that you show yourself.

19. Everything is now. The past is completely over, and the future is never yet. You are always arriving right where you are, and you are always at the right time and the right place. You have arrived.

20. Life is improv, that is, you are always making things up as you go along. You are always in a scene, whether you are alone or with another. The scene has its props, its actors, and its dialogue, and it will always develop on its own as it comes to completion.

21. You have never repeated the same scene twice.

22. You don't have to try to do anything but what you are already doing and be all that you are which takes no effort.

23. In doing this process, you are walking out of the prison of your thoughts. The door is the mirror.

24. Being the mirror, *("I am the mirror of existence"),* you identify with love itself.

About the Author

Cort is a practicing psychologist and author of several books on the subject of psychology, awareness and love.

Read more at https://www.presentcenteredtherapy.com.

About the Publisher

I am an independent publisher and author who writes books on psychology, awareness and love.